Southern and West Country Airfields of the D-Day Invasion Air Force

2nd Tactical Air Force in South and South-West England in WWII

Southern and West Country Airfields of the D-Day Invasion Air Force

2nd Tactical Air Force in South and South-West England in WWII

Peter Jacobs

Pen & Sword
AVIATION

First published in Great Britain in 2013 by
Pen & Sword Aviation
An imprint of Pen & Sword Books Ltd
47 Church Street
Barnsley
South Yorkshire
S70 2AS

ISBN 978 1 84415 901 7

A CIP catalogue record for this book is
available from the British Library

Typeset in 10pt Palatino by Mac Style, Driffield, East Yorkshire
Printed and bound in the UK by CPI Group (UK) Ltd,
Croydon, CRO 4YY

Pen & Sword Books Ltd incorporates the Imprints of Pen &
Sword Aviation, Pen & Sword Maritime, Pen & Sword Military,
Wharncliffe Local History, Pen & Sword Select, Pen & Sword
Military Classics, Leo Cooper, Remember When, Seaforth
Publishing and Frontline Publishing

For a complete list of Pen & Sword titles please contact
PEN & SWORD BOOKS LIMITED
47 Church Street, Barnsley, South Yorkshire, S70 2AS, England
E-mail: enquiries@pen-and-sword.co.uk
Website: www.pen-and-sword.co.uk

Contents

Acknowledgements

The story of these former wartime airfields could not have been told without the help of so many people. Some I have known and worked with over so many years such as the staffs at the RAF Museum, the Imperial War Museum, the National Archives and, in particular, the Air Historical Branch where I have always been so grateful for the continuous support of the head of the AHB, Seb Cox, and his team. They have all provided me with material and photographs over the years, much of which have helped me with this work and without the help of all these people stories such as this could never be told. In the case of the photographs and illustrations they are either from my own collection or have been included with the kind permission of either the AHB or, in some cases, individuals who have been credited accordingly.

While official sources are essential to military historians and authors alike, I never cease to be amazed by the kindness and help I receive from the local public who help preserve the legacy of these famous airfields, many of whom do so voluntarily. They deserve a personal mention because they all proved so helpful to me, sometimes through prior arrangement but mostly without any notification when they assisted me on the day. They are: Matt Sawday (Appledram); Mick Lambert, Tony Miles and Jo in the admin office at Blackbushe Airport (formerly Hartford Bridge); Phil Manning, Colin Watt and Robert Pollett (Lasham); the owner of the farm at Needs Oar Point who wishes to remain anonymous; Squadron Leader Ian Williamson (Odiham); Haydn Harvey (Thruxton); Mark Gibb and Simon Oliver at Goodwood Flying Club (formerly Westhampnett); Kevin Byrne and Yvonne Durell (Zeals). Thanks to them all.

Those I have mentioned in person are, without doubt, just the tip of the iceberg. Some of the sites I visited have memorials or museums to preserve the legacy of these former airfields or to remember those who served there during the Second World War. These memorials and museums have only been possible because of the vision and generosity of many people over the years and so, on behalf of everyone who appreciates what these people have done, I would like to thank them all.

Finally, but by no means least, I would like to thank Pen and Sword for giving me the opportunity to ensure these airfields are not forgotten and, in particular, to the late Peter Coles who I had the pleasure to work closely with over many years. He will be truly missed.

Introduction

My interest in old airfields dates back several years and I have been fortunate to be able to tell the brief histories of many of them, and the vital role they played during the Second World War, through this Aviation Heritage Trail Series. My first book on the subject, titled *Airfields of 11 Group* (published in 2005 and covering the period of the Battle of Britain), was followed in 2009 by *Airfields of the D-Day Invasion Air Force*, which covered the airfields in south-east England that were used by the 2nd Tactical Air Force (2nd TAF) during the period of the D-Day operations.

This latest work is a second volume on the airfields used by the 2nd TAF during the period of the D-Day operations and covers the twenty-one airfields in the south and south-west of England to add to the twenty-six airfields in the south-east that were covered in the previous volume; the boundary I have used between the two volumes is an imaginary line running south from Guildford to just east of Bognor Regis and so this book covers everything to the west of that line, from west Sussex to Cornwall.

Several airfields used by the 2nd TAF were only temporary and were designated as advanced landing grounds (ALGs) rather than given full airfield status. They had been identified as early as 1942 and were only to support the vast number of 2nd TAF squadrons, as well as American squadrons of the US Ninth Air Force, for a limited period during the build-up to the Allied invasion of Europe and immediately after. Each landing ground was constructed to a similar pattern with two metal track runways, a perimeter track and aircraft standings with a number of hangars and a facility for storing fuel.

Not all airfields used by the 2nd TAF during 1943–44 were involved in air operations over Normandy on D-Day – they were too far west and out of operational range of the invasion beaches – but all were used at one time during the period and so are included for completion; I have not, however, included those airfields or landing grounds that were used solely by the US Ninth Air Force during this period.

Some of these former wartime airfields and landing grounds, such as Hurn and Odiham, need little introduction. Hurn, for example, is now Bournemouth Airport and Odiham is one of the RAF's main operating bases and home to the Chinook helicopter. Some names are probably better known because of their coastal location – Bognor Regis, Lee-on-Solent, Perranporth and Selsey – where even many of the locals will not be aware that an airfield once existed. Other former airfields will be associated with other activities and these will include: Beaulieu (now a motor museum); Ford (as a prison); Thruxton (for its motor racing) and Westhampnett (now the Goodwood motor racing complex). Others will be unheard of other than to the most avid aviation historian or to those who have lived there; in this category I would include Appledram, Ibsley, Funtington, Needs Oar Point and Zeals.

To put the story about the airfields into some context, I have started the book with a brief insight into the 2nd TAF and the period covering the air operations in support of D-Day before looking at the airfields region by region. For each airfield I have given its brief history leading up to the period when the airfield was used by the 2nd TAF and then provided some brief exerts of what happened at the airfield immediately before, during and after D-Day. These often include mentions of just some of the gallant airmen who served at the airfield during the period, some of whom were highly decorated, and I have used the appropriate abbreviation when referring to their awards; DSO is the Distinguished Service Order, DFC the Distinguished Flying Cross and the Distinguished Flying Medal is abbreviated as DFM. At the end of each airfield I have provided a brief summary of the squadrons and aircraft types that served from the site during the period of interest.

Because of the number of airfields included in this work, I have chosen to cover each region in alphabetical order with the regions working from east to west throughout the book – from West Sussex, through Hampshire, Dorset and Wiltshire to Cornwall. For each airfield I have given directions for how to find it or to where the airfield once was, along with anything else of interest to see, and so I hope you find these useful should you wish to visit any of them for yourself. Only time and space prevents me from writing more and all I can hope to achieve is to provide you with a taste of each airfield's history and what is there today. I hope you enjoy the book.

CHAPTER ONE

The 2nd Tactical Air Force

As 1942 came to a close, the Royal Air Force found itself increasingly on the offensive in Europe and the pilots of Fighter Command were regularly flying fighter sweeps over enemy-occupied territory. Their previous role to defend mainland Britain had all but come to an end. Furthermore, given that Britain and her Allies were now fighting side by side in Europe, much thought had already been given as to how the air units should be organized during the vital period leading up to an Allied invasion of Europe and then, more importantly, during the vital months after. If Allied air units were expected to cross the Channel and operate effectively from the Continent then they would need to be placed on a mobile footing well in advance of their move and trials would need to be carried out to determine exactly how mobility would best be achieved.

There had previously been little in the way of joint operations between the RAF and the Army and the only previous organization regularly involved in such support was Army Co-Operation Command; this command had formed at the end of 1940 as the complexity of air power had started to increase but would now soon disband because the concept of army and air co-operation had changed radically. Exercise *Spartan*, which took place in March 1943, involving mainly British and Canadian forces, was the first exercise designed to test the concept of a composite group and airfield organization, and was one of the largest training exercises to involve both air and ground elements.

Exercise *Spartan* had proved invaluable but although air support of ground operations had been limited in the home theatre to a succession of exercises, the same could not be said of the North African theatre where air and land forces had fought in harmony for some time. Success in the desert now meant that more assets were available for the campaign in north-west Europe and, perhaps more importantly, the vast experience gained in the desert with the Desert Air Force, or the First Tactical Air Force, could be used to good effect and the composite groups operating in the Western Desert were considered suitable for adoption as a pattern for operations on the European Continent.

As preparations were made for the Allied invasion of mainland Europe, now looking to take place in the spring of 1944, it was increasingly evident that air power would be pivotal to success and this led to the existence of two well-equipped, and very powerful, tactical air forces: the United States Ninth Air Force and the RAF Second Tactical Air Force (2nd TAF). With the formation of the Allied Expeditionary Air Force (AEAF) on 13 November 1943, with its headquarters at Stanmore Park, both air forces would come under the command of Air Chief Marshal Sir Trafford Leigh-Mallory.

The announcement of Leigh-Mallory as Commander of the AEAF had been one of many announcements made at the end of 1943 that also included General Eisenhower to be the Supreme Allied Commander and that Air Chief Marshal Sir Arthur Tedder would be his Deputy Supreme Commander because of the vast contribution that air power would make if the Allies were to be successful in the invasion of Europe. Having commanded No. 12 Group during the Battle of Britain and then No. 11 Group and later Fighter Command, Leigh-Mallory had always believed that there should be a single commander of an Allied Air Force who would have overall command of individual commands, such as Fighter Command and Bomber Command, rather than there being a number of commanders all at the same rank. Although there would remain national rivalry, and national identities would remain, from this moment on operations would be combined such that the planning would be done together, as Allies and with the full co-operation of the single Services.

The earlier disbandment of Army Co-Operation Command had seen its units transferred to Fighter Command at about the same time as No. 2 Group, equipped with light and medium day bombers, had been transferred from Bomber Command. There had also been the formation of two new groups within Fighter Command; No. 83 Group with its headquarters at Gatton Park, Reigate, and No. 84 Group with its headquarters at Cowley Barracks, Oxford. These three groups formed the basis of the 2nd TAF following the disbandment of Fighter Command when its tactical elements became the 2nd TAF and its non-tactical elements reverted to the pre-1936 title of Air Defence of Great Britain (ADGB). This gave the AEAF three components: the US Ninth Air Force, ADGB and the 2nd TAF.

To some the disappearance of Fighter Command was considered a psychological blunder and would prove to be short-lived – as Fighter Command would return to the RAF's command structure less than a year later – but the decision to disband it had come about through necessity to prevent confusion. The RAF still had the responsibility of defending the UK but it also now needed to provide vital tactical air support to ground forces during the forthcoming invasion of Europe. Furthermore, the capabilities and roles of the later combat aircraft to enter service

Commander of the 2nd TAF, Air Marshal Sir Arthur Coningham (left), seen in discussion with the Deputy Supreme Allied Commander, Air Chief Marshal Sir Arthur Tedder (right). In the centre is Air Vice-Marshal Harry Broadhurst. (AOC No 83 Group)

merely added to the confusion; fighters were now also capable of carrying out a bombing or reconnaissance role. It showed how air warfare had changed so much and so quickly and so the decision was made to apportion Fighter Command's assets to ADGB and the 2nd TAF but it does highlight one of many changes made to organizational structures at the time.

The first commander of the 2nd TAF was Air Marshal Arthur Coningham. It was a natural and obvious choice. As commander of the Western Desert Air Force during 1942 he had championed the development of tactical air support for Allied troops on the ground. His leadership had been inspirational during victory in North Africa and he had subsequently directed operations during the invasion of Sicily and Italy.

The establishment of an extra headquarters in the Air Force chain of command would not be without its problems, and there would be testing times with Leigh-Mallory, but Coningham had experienced commanders beneath him. Commanding No. 2 Group was Air Vice-Marshal Basil Embry, who had already been awarded the DSO three times and he would subsequently fly nineteen operational sorties as an air-vice marshal, adding a fourth DSO while AOC No. 2 Group. Commanding No. 83 Group was Air Vice-Marshal Harry Broadhurst, who had just taken over the group from Air Vice-Marshal William Dickson and had previously served as the AOC Western Desert, and commanding No. 84 Group was Air Vice-Marshal Leslie Brown who had previous experience with Army cooperation and had been instrumental in helping to build-up the Desert Air Force. Furthermore, the commanders of the many wings and squadrons based in southern England were also vastly experienced.

At the time of its formation the headquarters of the 2nd TAF was located at Hartford Bridge. The 2nd TAF had been assigned fifty-four squadrons spread across twenty-one airfields. The largest of the three groups, in terms of the number of squadrons, was No. 83 Group with twenty-one squadrons across eight airfields: Biggin Hill, Kenley, Westhampnett, Gravesend, Detling, Gatwick, Merston and Redhill. The second largest was No. 84 Group with twenty squadrons located at eight airfields – Hornchurch, Northolt, Heston, North Weald, Ibsley, Fairlop, Odiham and Thruxton – and the smallest group, No. 2 Group, had eleven squadrons at five airfields: Hartford Bridge, Sculthorpe, Swanton

Morley, Dunsfold and Lasham. There were also two squadrons assigned to the headquarters at Hartford Bridge.

The fourth component of the 2nd TAF, No. 85 Group, formed at Uxbridge on 17 December 1943. Led by Air Vice-Marshal Cole-Hamilton, the group differed from the others of the 2nd TAF as it adopted a defensive posture, with its main roles being to provide air defence over the invasion build-up areas along the south coast of England and night defence of the 2nd TAF's airfields. The idea was that once the invasion took place then No. 85 Group would continue to provide night air defence over the Army's front-line units. Its headquarters at Uxbridge would soon move to nearby Hillingdon, a move that took place on 16 January 1944.

There then followed changes to the organization structure at the lower levels as airfields were given numbers. For example, Biggin Hill became No. 126 Airfield and Kenley became No. 127 Airfield, and the airfields were paired to form wings; for example, these two airfields became No. 17 Wing. However, the concept of numbered airfields did not last long and it would not be long before the organization's terminology would change again when, during the spring of 1944, each numbered airfield would become a wing; for example, No. 137 Airfield (Hartford Bridge) would become No. 137 Wing and No. 138 Airfield (Lasham) would become No. 138 Wing.

The wings were now commanded by a group captain and reported directly to their group. Although wings were nothing new as far as the RAF was concerned, the concept during the Second World War was somewhat different to the early days of wings during the First World War. The planners recognized the need for close air support during the forthcoming Allied invasion, which would require the combat aircraft of the 2nd TAF to operate from bases and airstrips as close to the front line as possible and to be able to react quickly as the ground forces advanced. Much had been learned from Exercise *Spartan* the previous year and the number of squadrons, aircraft and personnel within each wing varied from location to location depending on the size of the airfield and its facilities. The larger airfields could accommodate up to two wings of three squadrons each, whereas smaller airfields could only accommodate one squadron at a time.

The structure of numbered airfields and then wings was not always popular amongst the ground crews because they were usually assigned to the airfield or wing, rather than a particular squadron and so did not enjoy the same unit identity as the pilots. The squadrons were effectively split with the pilots and a small number of admin staff retaining the squadron number plate and the engineering ground crews were organized separately as servicing echelons; the idea being that the echelons could move quickly from airfield to airfield at short notice so as to service any aircraft that happened to arrive.

The 2nd TAF operated a number of different aircraft types. Essentially, the squadrons of Nos 83 and 84 Groups were equipped with Spitfires (Mark Vs and IXs), Mustangs (Mark Is and IAs), Hurricane IVs and Typhoon IAs, while No. 2 Group operated Mitchell IIs, Boston IIIs and Mosquito VIs. No. 85 Group was equipped with Mosquito XIII night-fighters and high-altitude Spitfire VIIs and XIVs to combat the enemy high-altitude reconnaissance aircraft that were flying over the likely invasion ports along the south coast of England.

Eighteen squadrons of the AEAF were equipped with the Typhoon, which was the RAF's chosen heavy fighter-bomber to support the Allied landings of north-west Europe, although the 400 or so aircraft assigned to these squadrons were of different modification states. The 2nd TAF had been keen to exploit the Typhoon's capability and during the early months of 1944 the aircraft's bomb load would be doubled and further modifications were made to deliver more explosives through a 'double-rocket' capability to increase the aircraft's firepower. The variation in roles, combined with the number of man hours required to re-configure an aircraft from a bomb-carrying to a rocket-armed capability, meant that squadrons usually specialized in one role and experience soon showed that pilots maintained a greater efficiency through constant practice. This resulted in the pilots of the ground-attack squadrons attending an Armament Practice Camp at Eastchurch, Llanbedr or Hutton Cranswick where they trained in either the fighter-bomber or rocket-firing roles.

While tactical air power was developing, the major offensive during the last months of 1943 and the early days of 1944 had been carried out by the heavy bomber force but now more and more medium-bomber attacks were being made, along with an increasing number of fighter sorties over north-west France, Belgium and Holland. These fighter sorties flown by the squadrons were given names such as *Rodeos* for fighter raids over enemy territory, *Rhubarbs* for low-level attacks on targets of opportunity, *Ramrods* for providing fighter escort for bombers and *Circus* for escorting medium bombers.

Gradually, the squadrons became increasingly involved in exercises with ground forces and there was less air combat training. It was not as if air-to-air combat training was considered unimportant, in fact many of the pilots were experienced fighter pilots, but many of the pilots had not been trained in air-to-ground techniques before and so there was further training in air-to-ground gunnery, rocket attacks and low-level bombing. Over the next few months the 2nd TAF built up in size and it would eventually grow to more than 100 squadrons spread across some fifty airfields.

The photo reconnaissance squadrons were busy across the Channel and were gathering vital information to help the planners in their task of preparing for the forthcoming Allied invasion of Europe. Also, the formation of the new Fighter Leaders' School at Milfield had seen the first course of students enter training. The aim of the course was to train and prepare wing leaders and squadron commanders in the fundamentals of ground-attack procedures, which would be vital when supporting the troops on the ground following the Allied invasion. The students on the first course included some of the RAF's finest fighter pilots such as Jamie Rankin, Billy Drake, George Keefer, Peter Wickham, Stanislaw Skalski, Reg Grant and Erik Haabjörn, after which the courses would include fighter pilots from all Allied nations.

In March 1944, General Montgomery was appointed as Commander-in-Chief of the Allied ground forces for the assault phase of Operation *Overlord*, a position equitable to Leigh-Mallory and their naval counterpart, Admiral Sir Bertram Ramsay, the Allied Naval Commander-in-Chief. Now, to ease the friction between the two air headquarters, Leigh-Mallory delegated operational control of the planning and operations of both the British and American tactical air forces to Coningham, now designated Commander Advanced Allied Expeditionary

Air Force (AEAF). The reason for the establishment of the Advanced AEAF, and Coningham as its commander, was to match the unified command of the ground forces with a unified command of the tactical air forces to ensure better cooperation during the final build-up to the Allied invasion and in the vital days that followed.

Coningham set up his headquarters at Hillingdon House, Uxbridge, so that he could easily attend meetings at the AEAF HQ at Bentley Priory while remaining close enough to his main HQ at Bracknell. Coningham was considered to be an excellent leader who knew how to get the best out of those around him. He not only understood the strategy of air warfare and its contribution to success on the ground but he also tried to visit as many of his units as he could so that he could meet the personnel under his command to gain a full appreciation of any problems at the lower levels of his organization.

The course of air operations had now changed. The combined offensive by Bomber Command and the US Eighth Air Force had now gathered momentum and an increasing number of American fighters, which were able to provide much-needed fighter escort for the American bombers operating by day, had been introduced. There were now larger formations of Allied bombers in the skies over Europe and the number of attacks against the V-1 'Noball' sites, which had been conducted as a matter of some priority since the New Year, was now being reduced as other targets became a priority during the final build-up to the Allied invasion.

Amongst the many wings of Nos 83 and 84 Groups, the various headquarters and units were moving to airfields along the south coast of England in preparation for the invasion and from where they would operate on D-Day. There were many moves and far too many to capture in detail, but during the month of April alone a total of sixteen airfield headquarters had moved location. But many of the airfields used by the 2nd TAF during its expansion were temporary and they were often poorly equipped. These were advanced landing grounds, or ALGs, which had been identified in southern England during the autumn of 1942 and then constructed during the following months. They were due to be completed by the spring of 1943, although many were completed significantly later.

Not all sites were given full airfield status and some became advanced landing grounds. These were not always capable of supporting operations all-year round, particularly in bad weather, and had metal runways laid, known as Sommerfeld tracks.

Twenty-three ALGs were allocated to the 2nd TAF and the USAAF, and had essentially been completed to the same pattern, although conditions locally had led to some necessary changes. The standard pattern was two metal Sommerfeld track runways, each typically 1,600 yards in length and fifty yards wide, with metal track aircraft standings and a perimeter track. Depending on the suitability of the site, there would be anything up to eight Blister-type hangars but apart from the hangars there would be very few buildings provided and so tents became the standard accommodation. The ground personnel were often required to set up temporary squadron accommodation and maintenance facilities around the edges of the airfield.

Coningham was keen to impress on his personnel that they were part of a mobile force with the main task of supporting forces on the ground. The experience he had gained from his time in the Western Desert stood him in good stead for turning his force into a mobile and expeditionary one. He was keen to ensure there were no thoughts of becoming static because once the invasion was under way he knew that his force would become, in his own words, a 'travelling circus'. And so he did not want his personnel to become too comfortable at their bases. The men and women soon found out what being part of a mobile force was all about!

At the beginning of April a new directive was issued stating that the time had come for the operations of the AEAF to be directed more closely to the preparation for *Overlord* and that the US Ninth Air Force had now been released from its overriding commitment of assisting the US Eighth Air Force's operations. The 2nd TAF and the US Ninth Air Force were now to conduct bombing operations against a prioritized list of targets. Whenever weather permitted the highest priority was the railway network and from May this would include the attacking of moving trains; this was something that had previously been prohibited on the grounds that the train might be carrying civilians. The second priority was the 'Noball' sites, the third priority was industrial targets and the fourth was enemy airfields. In the case of the enemy airfields, the intent was to deny the enemy the use of its airfields within 100 miles of the beachhead and, if possible, up to 130 miles, and during the final weeks before the invasion this was increased yet again to 150 miles and to destroy as much as possible the Luftwaffe's ability to maintain or repair its aircraft.

The destruction of rail facilities and rolling stock, especially locomotives, soon started to have a devastating effect on the Germans and it would eventually result in the termination of all non-military rail movements. This severely disrupted the movement of raw materials and supplies, and meant that manpower had to be diverted from other essential tasks to try and maintain the rail network. Furthermore, the crippling of the rail network meant that the Germans had to make greater use of the road network and this brought associated problems, such as slower transportation and increased fuel consumption.

Amidst the offensive operations it was vital to continue the strategic and tactical reconnaissance effort. Again, the main effort was prioritized with the main priorities being: to continue the visual and photographic reconnaissance of enemy dispositions and movements, particularly those that might affect the situation in the assault area; to conduct detailed reconnaissance of the enemy coastal defences and to detect the construction of any new defences; to continue observing the ports and to carry out a comprehensive photographic survey of prospective airfield sites in order to plan for the future build-up of air forces on the Continent. Each reconnaissance unit was heavily tasked as D-Day approached, as army commanders sought an increasing number of photographs of the landing beaches and the latest obstacles being prepared as part of the German defences.

The responsibilities of the different air headquarters had now been established. Understandably, Leigh-Mallory would initially co-ordinate the strategic elements of the air battle but once the invasion was fully underway then Coningham would also command the Advanced AEAF Headquarters until Leigh-Mallory could establish himself in France. It was also decided that No. 83 Group would support the Second British Army and No. 84 Group the First Canadian Army; both were major elements of the 21st Army Group and the main British and Commonwealth contribution to the Allied invasion force.

Leigh-Mallory's hopes that Coningham and Montgomery would work closely together on equal terms never seemed to materialize. Part of the problem seems to have stemmed from the fact that Montgomery did not see Coningham as an equal. Instead, he felt that he had two air force opposite numbers: Leigh-Mallory and Coningham. Equally, though, Leigh-Mallory did not insist that Montgomery work together with Coningham, rather than coming to himself on certain matters of strategic importance. Tedder, too, might have helped by making the position clear. The situation was not helped by the geographic locations of the commanders at the top. Montgomery was at Fort Southwick, near Portsmouth, Leigh-Mallory was at Stanmore and Coningham was at Uxbridge.

However, any problems between the commanders at the strategic level did not impact on operations at the tactical level. During the final weeks before the invasion the 2nd TAF turned its attention to destroying the German radar chain along the northern coast of France. The planners realized that this radar chain presented the biggest obstacle to the success of the Allied landings since the radar sites would be able to give the Germans vital warning time and completely destroy the Allied element of surprise. Similar to the British sites along the southern and eastern coastline of England, there were a number of German radars along the coast of northern France backed up by stations and sites situated further inland. There were too many sites to destroy them all but the aim was to neutralize as many as possible to give the Allies the element of surprise during the early hours of the invasion. From early May onwards a mix of rocket-armed Typhoons and bomb-carrying Typhoons and Spitfires were used, combined with the Allies using electronic counter-measures, against the sites. All six of the long-range reporting sites to the south of Boulogne were put out of action, so that large areas of the Channel were devoid of radar cover, and more than a dozen other sites were severely damaged to the extent that they were of no use to the Germans on D-Day.

Another major concern of the planners was the capability of the enemy's coastal batteries, which could create havoc along the coastline where the invasion was due to take place. The large 155mm guns that were located at some of the sites had a range in excess of 10 miles and this would mean that Allied shipping would be exposed to the coastal defences for two hours or more. Therefore it was essential that these sites were either destroyed or at least damaged to reduce their effectiveness. These hardened batteries could only be destroyed by a direct hit, which was considered extremely unlikely from bombing at height and so trials had been carried out using Typhoons against some of the more open emplacements, using both dive-bombing and rocket-firing techniques, and this showed some promise. In the end the best solution against the most hardened sites was using a combination of heavy bombing, rocket-firing and airborne forces to destroy any guns that had not already been put out of action.

Not only was there direct action against German targets that would need to be destroyed, or at least neutralized, prior to D-Day but the effort to deceive the Germans was maintained right up until the Allied invasion and for this purpose the use of air power was the key weapon. The sheer effort behind the Allied deception plan, and the subtlety and complexity in its execution, stands out as one of the remarkable achievements of *Overlord*. For every reconnaissance mission flown over Normandy there were two flown over the Pas de Calais and for every ton of bombs dropped on coastal batteries to the west of Le Havre, two tons were dropped on coastal batteries to the east,

The ground crews were often the unsung heroes of the 2nd TAF but worked tirelessly around the clock in the period leading up to, and during, the Allied invasion of Europe.

and for attacks against the railway system in northern France, 95 per cent of the effort was directed against targets north and east of the Seine.

There is no doubt the Germans were unaware of the imminence of the invasion until the very last few days, when German intelligence reports suggested that the intensity of the air attacks had convinced them that an attack was imminent, but not the location. The same intelligence reports stated that the deterioration in the transport system and constant attacks on bridges had prevented further constructional work on the coastal defences.

The total air effort during the build-up to D-Day had been immense. In the three months leading up to the invasion, one-third of the Allied strategic bombing effort, more than 60,000 tons, had been against transportation targets and of the remainder the majority had been against the German aircraft industry. During the final two months leading up to D-Day, the RAF had flown nearly 72,000 sorties of which the 2nd TAF had accounted for 28,600. The American Eighth and Ninth Air Forces had flown even more.

Now there assembled a vast organization of air assets available to the Supreme Commander of the Allied Forces, General Dwight D. Eisenhower. In addition to the 2nd TAF there were the tactical units of the US Ninth Air Force, mainly located at airfields in Kent, which combined to make a total of some 11,000 aircraft available to support the Allied invasion of Europe; more than 4,000 were British and nearly 7,000 American. Of the total number available, more than 4,000 were heavy bombers with a further 1,000 medium and light bombers, there were about 4,500 fighters and nearly 1,000 troop-carrying aircraft; the remainder were reconnaissance and air-sea rescue aircraft. There were also the fighter squadrons of No. 11 Group ADGB in the south-east of England. In terms of numbers, the overall Allied strength was a total of 630 squadrons; 254 were British and 376 American. Of the British strength, 96 squadrons, located at more than 30 airfields, were available to the 2nd TAF with the remainder belonging to Bomber Command and ADGB, which was still a substantial force for the defence of the homeland, particularly in the south and south-east from where the invasion would be launched. Of the American squadrons, nearly half were available to the US Ninth Air Force with the rest belonging to the US Eighth Air Force.

The Allied air plan involved more than 170 fighter squadrons with nearly one-third tasked with providing cover over the beaches. One-third was to carry out offensive air operations, including escort duties for bombers and airborne forces, and the remainder provided direct air support to the troops on the ground and air cover for Allied shipping. As far as air opposition was concerned, it was estimated that the Luftwaffe had about 500 aircraft available in the invasion area, only one-third of which comprised day fighters. The almost continuous bombardment of the Normandy region had meant that most of the Luftwaffe's *Jagdgruppen* had been withdrawn from airfields close to the northern coast of France.

In southern England, at airfields stretching from Cornwall in the far west, eastwards along the south coast and round the coast of East Anglia, the squadrons made their final preparations. The airfields of the 2nd TAF accommodated the bomber units of No. 2 Group, the fighter and fighter-bomber units of No. 83 Group and No. 84 Group, and the day-fighter and night-fighter units of No. 85 Group. The squadrons of Nos 83 and 84 Groups – twenty-four squadrons of Spitfire IXs, eighteen squadrons of Typhoon Is and six squadrons of Mustang IIIs, plus two reconnaissance wings – were mainly based at airfields stretching along the south coast, in the counties of West Sussex and Hampshire. The squadrons of No. 85 Group – another fourteen squadrons with the responsibility of providing air defence over southern England – were spread across the south and south-east, and the bombers of No. 2 Group – four squadrons of Mitchells, two of Bostons and six of Mosquitos – with greater range and endurance, were located at airfields more inland.

On 4 June all the 2nd TAF aircraft, as well as those of the US Ninth Air Force, were painted with black and white stripes. Although the markings would compromise the camouflage of the 2nd TAF's fighters and fighter-bombers, it would help the Allies identify friendly aircraft over the beaches once the invasion was underway. Immediately prior to the invasion the pilots were briefed not to fly too closely to land to ensure they did not highlight to the Germans that an offensive was imminent. This made air operations difficult during the final hours before D-Day, which was not helped by the subsequent delay of D-Day by twenty-four hours due to the weather.

While the 2nd TAF would play an enormous part in D-Day, it was just one part of an Allied armada of air, sea and land forces that would eventually liberate Europe. But the 2nd TAF was now ready to provide the vital air support for the greatest invasion in the history of warfare.

CHAPTER TWO

D-Day and Beyond

Almost four years to the day after the Royal Navy had rescued the remnants of the British Expeditionary Force from the beaches of Dunkirk, the greatest amphibious operation in history, Operation *Overlord*, took place on 6 June 1944. The Allies had assembled a fleet of nearly 7,000 ships and small craft of all types and an air armada in excess of 10,000 aircraft. Bad weather had seen southern England and the Channel experience a howling gale and heavy rain, which had led to a postponement of D-Day, originally set for 5 June, by twenty-four hours. Then, after a series of daunting weather

A Typhoon of No. 609 Squadron clearly showing the black and white stripes that were painted on Allied aircraft immediately prior to the D-Day landings.

forecasts by his meteorological experts, General Eisenhower was told that a break in the weather was coming, which was due to last for forty-eight hours, and so he gave the decision to 'go'.

The assault phase of the air campaign comprised six main elements: the protection of cross-Channel movement; the neutralization of coastal and beach defences; the air protection of the beaches; the dislocation of enemy communications and control; airborne operations; and the direct support of the land forces. During the night of 5/6 June, Bomber Command dispatched more than 1,200 sorties – a new record for the command – mainly against coastal batteries at Fontenay, Houlgate, La Pernelle, Longues, Maisy, Merville, Mont Fleury, Pointe-du-Hoc, Ousterham and St Martin-de-Varreville. There were also diversion attacks to conceal the true location of the invasion for as long as possible.

As the ships and craft set sail from their ports in southern England, it was the South-Western Approaches that faced the greatest menace from the U-boats that had threatened to cause havoc amongst the invasion fleet from their bases in the Bay of Biscay. While Coastal Command would later receive little recognition for its support to *Overlord*, its fifty squadrons would ensure that the invasion fleet enjoyed a safe passage across the Channel. For the squadrons of the 2nd TAF, personnel were informed of the imminent invasion during the early hours of 6 June. The obvious and immediate uplift in morale at the airfields along the south coast of England was there for all to see. The big day had finally arrived and everyone went about their task with a renewed energy and keenness to do their bit to make the day a great success.

The plan was to provide six squadrons of Spitfires at low-level over the landing beaches during the day, to complement a further seven American squadrons providing air cover over the beaches and Channel. Half of the eighteen Typhoon squadrons were to be tasked to attack specified targets and defensive positions, and the other half were to provide airborne alert over the invasion area; three squadrons were to cover each of the three eastern landing beaches of Gold, Juno and Sword. Three Mustang tactical reconnaissance squadrons and two squadrons of Spitfires, together with aircraft from the Air Spotting Pool, would help direct fire from the armada of ships positioned off the landing beaches and other squadrons would escort the mass airlift of gliders and troop-carrying aircraft. Once darkness fell then six squadrons of Mosquito night-fighters would provide night air cover over the invasion area.

Amongst the first Allied aircraft over the invasion area at about 5.00 a.m. were the 2nd TAF Bostons from Hartford Bridge, with the task of laying a smoke screen ahead of the first landing craft which were to hit the beaches a couple of hours later, and there were also a number of 2nd TAF tactical reconnaissance aircraft over the landing beaches and areas immediately inland. The first Allied landing craft went ashore shortly before 7.30 a.m. as the aircraft of the 2nd TAF carried out attacks against the German defences along the landing beaches, many of which were hardened. The first Typhoons over the invasion area were the Canadian squadrons of No. 143 Wing from Hurn, their arrival just before 7.30 a.m. coinciding with the first landing craft at the Gold, Sword and Juno beaches.

For the following few hours there was much confusion amongst the German High Command. This combined with the fact that the Luftwaffe units were spread across northern France, because of the uncertainty of where the invasion would come from and also because of the continuous bombardment of the Normandy area ahead of the invasion, and the adverse weather meant there was little in the way of air-to-air activity between the Allied fighters and the Luftwaffe during the early morning of D-Day.

Coningham had fully expected the Luftwaffe to have responded immediately, and in greater numbers, and from his perspective the lack of Luftwaffe activity during the early morning was a great bonus. But as the morning progressed the increasing amount of cloud cover over the invasion area made the 2nd TAF's task of preventing the enemy's movement on the ground all but impossible. The Luftwaffe managed to mount more and more sorties later in the day as the air battle intensified during the afternoon. There were successes on both sides and the 2nd TAF's Spitfire, Typhoon and Mustang squadrons all enjoyed some success. During the evening Mustangs from the 2nd TAF escorted the second wave of airborne troops, in gliders towed by tugs, across the Channel. Once it was dark it was the turn of the bombers of No. 2 Group to carry out night raids

The Typhoon equipped eighteen squadrons of the 2nd TAF in 1944 and was the RAF's specialist fighter-bomber to support the British and Allied troops advancing into north-west Europe.

against road and rail junctions and for the Mosquitos of No. 85 Group to conduct night intruder missions. Bomber Command also flew more than 1,000 sorties to add to the 1,200 sorties it had flown the night before.

The Allies flew more than 13,000 sorties on D-Day, of which some 2,200 sorties were flown by the 2nd TAF; ADGB flew about 1,000 sorties; Bomber Command flew nearly 1,500 sorties; Coastal Command and other RAF units also flew nearly 1,500 sorties; the US Eighth Air Force flew more than 4,000 sorties and the US Ninth Air Force flew more than 3,500 sorties. The total Allied effort included some 1,500 sorties flown by fighters to provide escort for bombers, troop-carrying aircraft or gliders, and more than 1,500 fighter sorties flown over the invasion beaches; throughout daylight hours there were up to 100 fighters providing fighter cover directly over the invasion beaches at any one time.

The squadrons of the 2nd TAF were mainly involved over the easterly landing beaches – Gold, Juno and Sword – where the British Second Army and Canadian First Army went ashore, although the 2nd TAF did maintain continuous fighter cover

over the Utah and Omaha beaches where American forces went ashore. In fact, more than one-third of the 2nd TAF sorties were flown as fighter cover over the beachhead and Allied shipping, with a further 500-plus sorties being flown as close air support, and nearly as many again providing artillery spotting. By the end of the day, the 2nd TAF's fighters had claimed seven of the twenty-eight enemy aircraft shot down by the Allies on D-Day and had claimed several more as either probably destroyed or damaged but the 2nd TAF had also lost eighteen aircraft during the first day.

There were times during D-Day when the unsuitable weather nullified to a certain extent the advantage enjoyed by the Allies of overwhelming air superiority. This was largely due to the fact that the heavy bombers could not operate effectively by day in such conditions. However, the Allied armies were ashore and reasonably well established, and the continuous round the clock air assault against German positions prevented the enemy from moving ground and air forces into key positions, and prevented a counter-attack during the first twenty-four hours of the Allied invasion.

One of the outstanding features of D-Day was the Allied air supremacy and it would remain that way for the rest of the war. The excellent co-ordination of the Allied air forces had provided an umbrella of security under which the ground forces could operate and the softening up of the enemy's defences by relentless attacks by the Allied bombers during the build-up to D-Day was now having a significant effect. While it would now be down to the landing forces on the ground to make the Allied invasion a success, it was possible for the Allied air forces, both strategic and tactical, to carry out their *Overlord* tasks with freedom while German forces had little or no movement in large areas of northern France and Belgium; the Allied plan to destroy, or at least severely disrupt, the transportation system had proved a great success. In fact, German strategy and tactics, combined with its fortifications and logistical problems, were all affected by the dominance of the Allied air power.

It was already evident that the landings on Gold beach in the west of the British sector had been extremely successful but things had not gone quite as well on Juno beach where the combination of the rough sea and the fact that many German defensive positions had survived the previous onslaught of the Allied bombing had meant there was more severe fighting. A gap between Juno and Sword beaches had allowed a German counter-attack during the evening but this, in turn, had been countered by the Allies and the German forces were pushed back. British and Canadian forces then made good progress inland, as did the Americans that had gone ashore on Utah beach, and by the end of D-Day a bridgehead some 5 miles deep had been established, although stiff German opposition in some key areas had meant the Allies were still, in some areas at least, short of their first day objectives.

The Allied air forces had laid the foundation of success by winning the air battle before the invasion had been launched and by applying their striking power with great effect to assist the landings. Furthermore, the disruption of the enemy's communications caused by the air campaign, combined with the breakdown of its radar capability through bombing and counter-measures, had left the enemy for some considerable time in doubt about the actual strength of the Allied assault.

The immediate post-landing tasks now were to link the bridgeheads, retain the initiative and to guard against any setbacks or reverses. Bomber Command again dispatched more than a thousand sorties during the night, concentrating on communications targets such as railway junctions and roads behind the Normandy battle area. The following day, 7 June, was a busy one for the 2nd TAF squadrons and alongside the successes there were the inevitable losses with thirty-six aircraft lost; a mix of Spitfires, Seafires, Typhoons and Mustangs. The Americans had also suffered losses with more than forty aircraft lost. However, the Allied fighters had made significant claims against the Luftwaffe, including the 2nd TAF's claims of thirty-four enemy aircraft to add to the American claims of forty-one enemy aircraft destroyed. Then, during the night after D-Day, the RAF night-fighters were out in force, although the majority of the ten enemy aircraft claimed as destroyed came from No. 11 Group aircraft with only one success from the 2nd TAF units.

So far the German reaction to the invasion had been relatively slow but more enemy troops were now gradually arriving in the area but not yet in enough numbers or strength for the Germans to launch a significant counter-attack. Throughout the day

Ground personnel taking a well-earned break during the high-tempo period of operations that followed the Allied invasion of Europe.

the weather had interfered with the Allied flying programme, which frustrated Leigh-Mallory because he could often not carry out the required bombing against German reinforcements by daylight. He felt that the Allies were losing precious time and this was just at a time when the enemy's main movements were beginning to take effect. But Leigh-Mallory also acknowledged that the Allies had enjoyed a relatively easy run as far as the Luftwaffe was concerned and he now wanted to take advantage of this and hit it as hard as possible.

The situation was much the same for the Allies on 8 June as it had been on the previous day by which time considerable reinforcements and a further hundred enemy aircraft had now arrived in the area. However, the Luftwaffe's tactics of using these aircraft in the fighter-bomber role, rather than purely a fighter role, is subject to some criticism; if they had been allowed to hassle the Allied aircraft more, rather than being hassled themselves, in particular by the Spitfire IXs, losses to the 2nd TAF units during the first days after the Allied landings might well have been higher.

Leigh-Mallory now considered the situation was changing considerably as more and more German reinforcements reached the invasion area. The weather was still deteriorating but the Allied fighter-bombers had managed to delay the enemy's movements and he was now keen to secure a ring outside the invasion area and to stop further railway movements towards the area, particularly from the south-east. He also wanted to take out any bridges and by doing so this would force the enemy onto the roads and this, in turn, would further delay reinforcements. He was also now concerned that the Luftwaffe activity was increasing and intelligence suggested that half of the fighters in Germany were now moving up to the invasion area and he wanted to hit the Luftwaffe while it was still on the move.

The weather had deteriorated significantly by 9 June, which resulted in a considerable reduction in Allied sorties flown, and at times it brought air operations to a halt, although by the evening the weather had improved sufficiently to allow some night operations to take place. During the days that followed the 2nd TAF squadrons were almost continuously in action from first light whenever the weather permitted. The Mustangs and Spitfires maintained near-continuous photo-reconnaissance cover of the Normandy area, much of which was carried out with extreme bravery when operating at tree-top height and at times in poor visibility, to continuously provide information about the situation on the ground while the bomb-carrying Mustangs attacked roads approaching the invasion area. The demand for Typhoon support for the advancing troops on the ground continued to increase – resulting in an increase in the number of Typhoon sorties during the following days – and the Spitfires continued to provide air cover over the invasion area. However, Luftwaffe activity had increased, and German positions were now being reinforced, and so came an increase in Allied losses, particularly as a result of an increase in German ground defences. This led to more attacks against the German airfields, which would eventually result in pushing the Luftwaffe further and further back.

In the days immediately after D-Day the Allies task was to secure its foothold in Normandy and to widen its bridgehead to allow further reinforcements before attempting to break out from the beachhead into northern France. By 12 June all the beachheads had been linked into one long continuous bridgehead with a front of 50 miles and a depth of up to 12 miles in places. Although the weather and heavy seas had caused problems with the logistical effort, the overall strategy was working well and it now remained for the defensive sector to hold against the increasing weight of opposition.

Air power was as important as ever, including the tactical use of strategic bomber forces. While Bomber Command concentrated on the bigger and more heavily constructed targets, for example the Saumur railway tunnel, which was attacked by Lancasters two nights after D-Day, the fighter-bomber squadrons of the 2nd TAF were tasked with attacking the smaller pin-point targets, such as bridges, as well as attacking locomotives and rolling stock on the move to try and reinforce German defensive positions in the invasion area, and key targets such as radar sites. The squadrons of No. 2 Group were equally active, where the Boston IIIs were now being replaced by B-25 Mitchells, and one example was an attack against the headquarters of the commander of Panzer Group West, General Geyr von Schweppenburg, which was located in the Chateau de la Caine to the south-west of Caen. The attack was carried out during the evening of 10 June by more than seventy Mitchells from No. 2 Group, bombing from medium level, with more than forty rocket-firing Typhoons from Hurn and Holmsley South operating at low-level, which resulted in the destruction of communications and signals equipment as well as destroying many vehicles located in the grounds of the chateau where the headquarters was situated; it would be more than two weeks before the headquarters would be fully functional again.

The 2nd TAF was tasked with slowing down the German reinforcements in order to prevent them from reaching the invasion area or to at least delay them as much as possible. The German belief that the main invasion would happen in the Pas de Calais meant that the two German army groups in the region, Army Group B, under the command of *Feldmarschall* Erwin Rommel, and Army Group G, under the command of *Generaloberst* Johannes Blaskowitz, were spread across a wide area and there was still some reluctance to commit significant German forces to the defence of Normandy, although for Coningham this, in turn, created some uncertainty about the intent of the Luftwaffe.

The deterioration in weather had allowed the occasional rest and a chance to carry out essential maintenance of the aircraft but it was never possible to maintain the amount of effort for very long. The plan had always been to get the fighters and ground crew across the Channel as soon as possible and once the Allies had secured the bridgehead and their foothold in Normandy, one of the next tasks was to construct landing strips for fighters. Amongst the first to have gone ashore in the immediate days after D-Day were personnel from the airfield construction wings and the construction of landing strips commenced in order of priority. Initial construction was to focus on providing emergency landing strips for the Allied fighters operating over Normandy. This would be followed by the construction of re-fuelling and re-arming strips to enable a quick turn-round of fighters on the ground rather than the fighters having to return to their bases in southern England; this would make a vast difference to the amount of time each fighter could spend on task during the hours of daylight, although the fighters would return to their home bases at dusk or for any damage repair or maintenance. The third priority was the construction of advanced landing grounds along similar lines to those constructed in southern England. The requirement was for a runway strip of between 1,000 yards and 1,700 yards depending on the type of aircraft that would operate from the site. The runway was generally constructed of square mesh track, or SMT as it was known, which had been developed from the Sommerfeld track.

During the detailed planning for the Allied invasion, the planners had hoped that by D+3 (three days after D-Day, i.e. 9 June) there would be four re-fuelling and re-arming strips available for use and by D+10 there would be ten fully constructed ALGs (five British and five American). This number should have grown to eighteen ALGs (ten British and eight American) by D+14 and by D+24 there would be twenty-seven ALGs (fifteen British and twelve American). However, in reality it would prove to be quite different. Progress on the ground was often slow as German resistance intensified but once the Allied advance started to gather momentum, and the ALGs were being completed one by one, Coningham was able to start moving the operational wings across the Channel.

The first landing ground at Asnelles-sur-Mer, just inland from Gold beach, was completed in remarkably quick time and was available as an emergency landing ground within forty-eight hours of the first troops going ashore. The airfield was simply designated as B.1 with the 'B' standing for British (American airfields were designated 'A') and the airfields numbered in sequence following completion. The emergency landing strip at Asnelles-sur-Mer had a short runway of just 600 yards and was only ever intended to be an emergency landing ground until longer and better prepared landing strips became available, after which Asnelles-sur-Mer would be used as a storage base for crashed aircraft.

From 12 June the landing grounds at Banville (B.2) and St Croix-sur-Mer (B.3) were ready for use by the 2nd TAF's Spitfires and Typhoons. These were longer runways (1,700 yards and 1,200 yards respectively) but the landing grounds were not yet ready to receive squadrons on a more permanent basis and so the initial idea was for the fighters and fighter-bombers to fly in at first light and then to carry out several operations before returning to their home bases in southern England at dusk.

However, delays in consolidating the bridgehead and then expanding it prevented vital equipment from going ashore and the planned number of ALGs to be available by certain dates would be quite different to what the planners had previously estimated. Instead of there being ten ALGs available by 16 June (D+10), there were in fact six available and by 25 June (D+19) there were eleven rather than the twenty that had been planned.

Operating from these temporary landing strips was never straightforward and the rough and rugged surfaces, which created clouds of dust and other surface debris, meant that aircraft engines suffered far more than normal; none more so than in the case of the Typhoon where the number of engine changes required were significantly higher than normal and a temporary modification to cover the carburettor air intake had to be installed.

The day of 18 June marked significant progress by the Allies on its western flank when advancing US troops linked up with British troops to cut off German forces defending the port of Cherbourg. This now meant that the Allies would soon be in a position to capture a major port but on its eastern flank the advance had all but stalled around Caen. Rather unexpectedly a strong gale blew up in the Channel during the early hours of 19 June, which brought daylight flying operations virtually to a standstill for the following three days. There was considerable damage to the Mulberry harbours, which were still under construction, and the American harbour at St Laurent had been destroyed, while the British harbour at Arromanches had been severely damaged. Furthermore, hundreds of ships at sea had been damaged or stranded.

Following the storm the first two full days of operations, on 22 and 23 June, were intense and hard fought in the skies over Normandy. But the storm, which was the worst suffered in the Channel for some forty years, had meant that the planned British offensive had to be postponed and Operation *Epsom*, the plan to capture Caen and the surrounding countryside, did not commence until 25 June, although two more days of poor weather, 26 and 27 June, further restricted the amount of close air support the 2nd TAF could provide in support of *Epsom*.

By the end of June nearly 900,000 Allied troops had been landed in Normandy. Apart from the loss of some units to counter the V-1 threat now faced in southern England, the composition of the 2nd TAF had changed little, although the basing of the squadrons had changed considerably. Many 2nd TAF squadrons had now crossed the Channel and were now operating from airstrips in Normandy. Capturing the ground would be vital to the construction of more temporary airfields and, despite strong German resistance, further operations, *Charnwood* and *Goodwood*, launched on 7 July and 18 July respectively, meant that the Allies were slowly able to break out of Normandy.

Although the construction of airfields was slower than planned, and occasionally proved frustrating for the Allied commanders, it never became a major issue and eventually there would be 220 airfields constructed in north-west Europe of which 150 were British and seventy American. Furthermore, as the Allies advanced, more and more enemy airfields were captured and once any attempts to sabotage the airfield had been removed or repaired, these airfields were also made available for use.

As the Allies advanced Coningham gave the role of maintaining air superiority ahead of the army columns, and to provide valuable close air support, to No. 83 Group that was operating with the Second British Army. No. 84 Group, which had been working with the First Canadian Army, was given the task of protecting the western flank of the advance as well as providing support to the combined operations tasked with capturing the ports between Le Havre and Antwerp.

On 5 August the Advanced AEAF ceased to exist, as it was no longer required, and Coningham reverted to commanding the 2nd TAF. There had been sufficient advance to allow him to move his 2nd TAF Headquarters across the Channel to Le Tronquay, to the south of Bayeux, and then to Amiens and then Brussels to keep up with the advance. By the end of September the Allies had come up against the natural barriers of the major rivers, which for the time being prevented any further advance. Then, with the Allies safely established on mainland Europe, and with a new threat of V-1 flying bombs now being increasingly launched against London, the first of which had been seen over southern England during the night of 14/15 June, combined with opportunity attacks by the Luftwaffe, the decision was made to reform Fighter Command on 15 October 1944 and ADGB was disbanded once more.

CHAPTER THREE

Airfields and Advanced Landing Grounds of West Sussex

The county of Sussex has had a strong connection with aviation since its birth some 100 years ago. Its location in the south of England, combined with its close proximity to London, made the county popular for aviation enthusiasts during its early days and the county has been home to many airfields over the years. This chapter covers those airfields and advanced landing grounds that were used by the 2nd TAF during 1943–44 and that lie to the west of Worthing. Some of the airfields, such as Tangmere and Thorney Island, will need little introduction to the aviation enthusiast or RAF historian, whereas Westhampnett might be better known to some as Goodwood. The names of others – for example Ford, Selsey and Bognor Regis – might be better known as a prison, landmark or coastal town rather than as airfields, and one or two, such as Appledram or Funtington, might not be known at all.

Of the airfields and landing grounds covered in this chapter, the only one still used actively for flying is Goodwood, formerly called Westhampnett. Of the others, Thorney Island was retained by the RAF for many years until it was handed over to the Army and the history of Tangmere has been preserved through the Tangmere Military Aviation Museum. The rest have effectively disappeared back to Sussex countryside or have been developed in some other way and few, if any, reminders of these former airfields remain. However, the close proximity of these former airfields to each other suggests that the airspace along the coastline of West Sussex was probably quite busy during the Second World War!

Appledram or Apuldram

Appledram, also found spelt as Apuldram, is a small parish on the north-eastern upper reach of Chichester Harbour, about 2 miles to the south-west of the West Sussex town of Chichester. It has always been an area of natural beauty but in 1944 it was a hive of activity during the D-Day period when it was home to a Czech wing of Spitfires.

The origins of this airfield date back to 1942 when, as part of a large programme to identify possible sites for the development of airfields along the south coast of England, a suitable location was identified on a large grass area of farmland at Manor Farm near the village of Appledram. The site was then chosen for the development of an advanced landing ground and work commenced early the following year. Two Sommerfeld track runways, which were made up of heavy steel netting held rigid, were laid at ninety degrees to each other. The main runway followed the standard pattern length of approximately 1,600 yards and was orientated south-west to north-east, and the second runway, running south-east to north-west, was slightly shorter at around 1,400 yards in length.

Typhoon fighter-bombers of No. 124 Airfield were the early occupants at Appledram when it opened as an advanced landing ground in June 1943.

Like at all ALGs, facilities at Appledram were only ever meant to be temporary, particularly as far as accommodation was concerned, where tents were the norm, although some local buildings, including farm houses, were later requisitioned for use. Other temporary facilities included metal hardstandings, a perimeter track and two Blister hangars for aircraft maintenance. The local farmers, however, were still permitted to graze their sheep when the airfield was not in use.

Work at the ALGs had to be completed by the spring of 1943 and the airfield was ready in time for the first fighter-bomber aircraft to arrive at the beginning of June. Three squadrons of Typhoons of the newly formed No. 124 Airfield moved in from Lasham in Hampshire on 2 June 1943 and the area suddenly came to life. As with all ALGs, the facilities at the site were very basic; tents for the squadron personnel and the Typhoons were quickly dispersed around the airfield. Two of the squadrons – Nos 181 and 182 Squadrons – had been operating the Typhoon since September 1942 and had been carrying out attacks against enemy coastal shipping and, more recently, targets in northern France. Appledram was their seventh home in just nine months. The third squadron, No. 175 Squadron, had only just taken delivery of the Typhoon a few weeks earlier, having previously operated the Hurricane II, and were still working up with the new type.

The first cross-Channel raids by the Typhoons of Appledram were flown during mid-June, mainly against enemy airfields in France and against other communications targets. No. 175 Squadron flew its first operational sorties with the Typhoon on 12 June against the airfield at Abbeville. However, the Typhoons did not stay long because those early days were merely to test the capability of Appledram as an ALG, and by early July all the aircraft had moved to airfields in Kent; Nos 181 and 182 Squadrons stayed together and moved to New Romney and No. 175 Squadron moved to Lydd. Appledram then became a standby airfield but further preparations began to take place for the arrival of more aircraft in the build-up to the Allied invasion of Europe. Four additional Blister hangars were erected for aircraft maintenance and more metal hardstandings put in place.

Improvements to the ALGs had to be completed by the beginning of April 1944 and within a few days Appledram was

A Spitfire IX of No. 313 Squadron at Appledram prior to the Allied invasion. The airfield's basic facilities are evident in the background.

home to three squadrons of Spitfire IXs of No. 134 Airfield, No. 84 Group, which moved in from Mendlesham. The first squadron to arrive was No. 310 Squadron on 3 April, followed the next day by the arrival of Nos 312 and 313 Squadrons. Operations commenced soon after, which included fighter sweeps and fighter escort for bombers attacking targets in northern France.

During the evening of 5 June the pilots were briefed on the part they were about to play during the following day, D-Day. Early the following morning, 6 June, the Czech squadrons were placed on thirty-minute readiness. Their task was to provide air cover for the British and Canadian forces landing on the eastern sector of the beaches and throughout the day the Appledram Spitfires were involved in air patrols over the beaches and surrounding areas without significant incident, with the Czech squadrons flying more operational sorties on 6 June than any other unit.

In the two weeks after D-Day the Czech squadrons enjoyed some success against the Luftwaffe. One example was during the early afternoon on 8 June when the Czech squadrons of No. 134 Wing, led by the wing leader, Wing Commander J Cermak, were operating over the invasion beaches. It was their second patrol of the day when they encountered several Focke-Wulf FW190 fighter-bombers bombing the beaches. During the aerial combat that followed, Cermak gave chase and shot down one of the FW190s some 15 miles to the south-east of Caen. During the encounter, which lasted just a matter of a few minutes, the pilots of the Czech squadrons claimed three FW190s destroyed and a further five as damaged; no Spitfires were lost.

The weather then deteriorated on 9 June, which resulted in a significant reduction in Allied sorties flown and at times brought air operations to a halt. The Czech squadrons were then transferred to ADGB and moved to Tangmere to conduct air patrols against the V-1 rocket threat, known as anti-Diver patrols. They were replaced at Appledram by a Polish wing, No. 131 Wing, also equipped with Spitfire IXs, which almost immediately commenced operations in support of the Allied breakout of Normandy. With an Allied foothold in Europe now all but secure, the wing moved to Ford on 16 July in preparation for deployment across the Channel. Appledram was no longer used as an airfield and by the beginning of 1945 the runways and hangars had been removed as the land reverted to agriculture.

The site of the former airfield is on the land of the Apuldram Manor Farm, a 650-acre arable and dairy farm in an area of outstanding natural beauty. Few signs of this former airfield have survived to the present day but the site can be found from the A27 by following the A286 Stockbridge Road south-westwards towards the village of Apuldram, which then becomes Birdham Road. After about 2 miles, as the road bears left in a more southerly direction, turn right into Dell Quay Road towards the

A Spitfire IX of No. 310 Squadron having its guns tested. This squadron operated from Appledram as a fighter-bomber unit throughout the period of the D-Day operations.

Dell Quay Sailing Club. This road, which runs westwards, cuts across what was the northern part of the airfield; both runways were to the south of the road but the road had to be closed off during the period when the airfield was active.

The houses at the western end of Dell Quay Road mark the north-western corner of the former airfield and this is where the north-western threshold of the secondary runway, which ran down to the south-east, once was. Returning back eastwards along Dell Quay Road you will soon see a track leading down to the right known as Salterns Way, which is a cycle way that runs from Chichester through the fields in Appledram to the sand dunes of East Head. About two hundred yards down the track on the right is an information board with more information about the former airfield, and at this point you are not too far from where the two runways once intersected; the main runway ran from the south-west at an area known as Salterns Copse, which is almost at the point where the Chichester Canal meets the estuary, through a point approximately where you are now standing and north-

Looking north-west from Salterns Way across the former site of Appledram and from a position not too far from where the two runways would have crossed. The small group of buildings in the distance mark the north-west part of the airfield from where the secondary runway ran towards the south-east. The main runway, which ran from the south-west to the north-east, would have run left to right across this view.

eastwards as far as the A286 Birdham Road. The farm buildings that you can see to the south, further down the Salterns Way, mark the location of what was one of the technical sites; there were others at the southern end of the airfield, the eastern end of the airfield and in the north-west part of the airfield.

Having returned back up the track to Dell Quay Road, you will see at the crossroads that the track continues northwards to Apuldram Manor Farm but this becomes a private track on the north side of the road. However, you can clearly see the buildings of the farm and they mark the location of one of the two domestic sites. If you now return eastwards down Dell Quay Road, and shortly before rejoining the A286, you will see Appledram Lane to the left. Although tents were mainly used for accommodation, the buildings mark the location of the second domestic site and if you proceed northwards along Appledram Lane there were some buildings located adjacent to the sharp right-hand bend and many of the nearby cottages were also requisitioned for accommodation.

Squadron	Dates at Appledram	Aircraft type
175 Squadron	2 Jun–1 Jul 43	Typhoon I
181 Squadron	2 Jun–2 Jul 43	Typhoon I
182 Squadron	2 Jun–2 Jul 43	Typhoon I
310 (Czech) Squadron	3 Apr–22 Jun 44	Spitfire IX
312 (Czech) Squadron	4 Apr–22 Jun 44	Spitfire IX
313 (Czech) Squadron	4 Apr–22 Jun 44	Spitfire IX
302 'Poznanski' Squadron	28 Jun–16 Jul 44	Spitfire IX
308 'Krakowski' Squadron	28 Jun–16 Jul 44	Spitfire IX
317 'Wilenski' Squadron	28 Jun–16 Jul 44	Spitfire IX

Bognor Regis

The area is now a popular holiday destination for those visiting the seaside town of Bognor Regis but there was once an airfield just over a mile to the north-east of the town that was home to Spitfires of No. 132 Wing during D-Day. The origins of this airfield date back to the late 1920s when there had been plans for a municipal airport. In the end the airport never happened and

The airfield at Bognor Regis opened in June 1943 and was home to Spitfires during the period of the D-Day operations.

the land previously identified was built on for housing but the fact that the area had been identified as suitable for development became important during the Second World War when agricultural land adjacent to the previous site was identified as suitable for development as an advanced landing ground.

Work commenced in early 1943 and the construction followed the standard ALG template with two Sommerfeld tracks laid at right-angles; one runway ran from the south-west to the north-east and the other from the south-east to the north-west. The airfield opened at the beginning of June 1943 and was administered by nearby Tangmere.

The first aircraft to operate from the new site were Spitfires of Nos 122 and 602 Squadrons of No. 122 Airfield, which moved in to Bognor at the end of June. They were soon joined by the Spitfires of No. 19 Squadron and the three squadrons took part in fighter sweeps across the Channel.

Having proved that Bognor Regis was suitable as an ALG, the aircraft of No. 122 Airfield moved out at the beginning of July. There followed further construction at the site, including the construction of additional hangars, hardstandings and taxiways. There was no flying from the site until No. 132 Airfield, part of No. 84 Group 2nd TAF, moved to Bognor Regis from North Weald at the end of March 1944 to begin its work-up as a Spitfire IX wing for fighter-bomber duties. The wing consisted of three squadrons – Nos 66, 331 and 332 Squadrons – and commenced operations in April and during their first Ranger against Juvincourt airfield, near Paris, on 11 April, No. 332 Squadron destroyed six enemy aircraft.

The Spitfires of No. 66 Squadron spent the latter part of April and the early part of May away from Bognor, first to Southend for an armament practice camp and then to Castletown. The squadron was now led by Squadron Leader Hugh Johnston, more commonly known as either 'Tim' or 'Johnny', who had previously served in the heroic defence of Malta for which he had been awarded a DFC, and by the time Johnston assumed command of No. 66 Squadron in May 1944 he had been awarded a bar to his DFC.

The three squadrons continued to take part in fighter sweeps across the Channel, as well as attacks against V-1 sites, and then during the period of D-Day operations the wing flew patrols over the invasion area. The weather then deteriorated on 9 June, which resulted in a significant reduction in Allied sorties flown and at times brought air operations to a halt. However, once the weather had improved, operations soon resumed but sadly, during the evening, the commanding officer of No. 331 Squadron, Major Leif Lundsten, was shot down by fire believed to have been from American ships and was killed.

The Spitfires of No. 132 Wing enjoyed considerable success during an early morning fighter sweep over Dieppe on 15 June when they encountered a mix of twenty or more Messerschmitt Bf109s and Focke-Wulf FW190s in the Evreux area. The thirty-six Spitfires, led by the Norwegian ace Lieutenant Colonel Rolfe Berg, had taken off from Bognor at first light and engaged the Bf109s and FW190s at 10,000 feet soon after 6.30 a.m. During the aerial engagement that followed, the Bognor wing shot down eight of the enemy aircraft and claimed damage to at least a dozen more; one Spitfire was lost. Three of the kills were credited to pilots of No. 332 Squadron and three to the pilots of No. 66 Squadron, including one to the commanding officer, 'Tim' Johnston, with the other two falling to the guns of No. 331 Squadron. It was a great morning for the wing. Sadly, however, Rolfe Berg, who had led the wing that morning and had been awarded a bar to his DFC and a DSO for leading No. 132 Wing, would not survive the war; he was shot down by flak over Holland in February 1945 and was killed.

Completely unexpectedly a strong gale blew up in the Channel during the early hours of 19 June, which brought daylight operations to a standstill for the following three days. No. 132 Wing then moved to Tangmere on 21 June and No. 83 Group Support Unit moved in to Bognor from Redhill. The Support Unit was a mass pool of a hundred reserve aircraft – consisting of Spitfires, Typhoons and Mustangs – and with a reserve pool of pilots. With an increasing number of V-1 rocket attacks against London, many were falling short of their target and Redhill was right beneath the flight path of the V-1s and so the Support Unit was considered vulnerable; hence the decision to move it to Bognor.

Bognor Regis was also used by Ansons of No. 1310 Flight, which were used as air ambulances to carry blood into the area of the bridgehead in support of the Allied break out of Normandy and the subsequent advance towards Germany. No. 83 Group Support Unit then moved to Thorney Island in September and flying ceased from Bognor. By early 1945 the runways had been removed and the site reverted to agriculture, although an airstrip of 600 yards was laid out and used by Longford Engineering, which later became LEC Refrigeration, until 1993.

The site of the former airfield is not easily accessible but can be found to the north of the town of Bognor Regis and to the east of the A29 Shripney Road, with the railway line that runs from Bognor northwards to Barnham marking the western boundary of the former airfield and Bognor Regis Golf Club marking the eastern boundary; the airstrip, which runs south-west to north-east, lies between the railway line and the golf course. A large housing estate on the eastern side of the A29 at South Bersted marks the southern edge of the former airfield.

Squadron	Dates at Bognor Regis	Aircraft type
122 Squadron	1 Jun–1 Jul 43	Spitfire V
602 Squadron	1 Jun–1 Jul 43	Spitfire V
19 Squadron	26 Jun–2 Jul 43	Spitfire V
66 Squadron	31 Mar–22 Jun 44	Spitfire IX
331 (Norwegian) Squadron	31 Mar–22 Jun 44	Spitfire IX
332 (Norwegian) Squadron	31 Mar–21 Jun 44	Spitfire IX

Ford

Now the site of an industrial estate and Her Majesty's Prison Ford, this airfield was used extensively by the 2nd TAF during 1944 in support of the Allied invasion of Europe. First developed in 1917 the airfield was originally known as Ford Junction but was also locally referred to as Yapton. The airfield was used by the Royal Flying Corps and the Americans during the latter stages of the First World War but the airfield closed in 1920.

The site was reactivated during the early 1930s and used by various aviation companies and at one time was used by the Ford motor company. In 1937 the airfield became RAF Ford as part of Coastal Command but it was then transferred to the Admiralty in May 1939 and commissioned as HMS *Peregrine*. The airfield was used by a number of Royal Navy squadrons and training units during the opening months of the Second World War. In August 1940 the airfield came under heavy attack from the Luftwaffe and sustained significant damage because the Germans believed that Ford was one of the RAF's main operating bases during the Battle of Britain. The following month Blenheims moved in to operate in the night-fighter role and the airfield was transferred to the RAF as part of No. 11 Group, Fighter Command. There were further raids against Ford during October but these were

Two wings of Spitfire IXs of No. 83 Group – No. 125 Wing and No. 144 Wing – operated from Ford in support of the D-Day landings.

all quite minor when compared with the heavier attacks carried out by the Luftwaffe only a few weeks earlier.

The last naval unit left Ford at the end of 1940 and the Fighter Interception Unit, equipped with Blenheims and Beaufighters, moved in from Shoreham. By 1942 the airfield had been further developed with the construction of two tarmac runways, one of 2,000 yards in length that ran from the south-west to the north-east and the other of 1,600 yards running from the south-east to the north-west, and the construction of permanent taxiways and hangars.

Several squadrons came and went during 1943 and by early 1944 Ford was home to Mosquito night-fighters. The airfield was then prepared for the arrival of the first 2nd TAF aircraft and Mustangs of No. 122 Airfield arrived from Gravesend on 15 April. The three squadrons – Nos 19, 65 and 122 Squadrons – immediately commenced offensive fighter operations across the Channel. They were soon joined by Spitfires of No. 125 Airfield – consisting of Nos 132, 453 and 602 Squadrons – which arrived from Detling and immediately commenced fighter sweeps across northern France and the Low Countries, as well as carrying out fighter escort for bombers.

Leading No. 132 Squadron at the time was Squadron Leader Geoffrey Page who had been given command of the squadron earlier in the year. Born in Hertfordshire, Page was amongst the most courageous of all the fighter pilots to have served with the RAF during the Second World War. He was just twenty-three years old when he was in command of No. 132 Squadron but, by then, he had already suffered such personal suffering when, during the Battle of Britain, he had served as a young twenty-year old Hurricane pilot with No. 56 Squadron and had scored his first success of the war. However, his involvement in the battle was cut short in August 1940 when he was shot down during an attack against a formation of Dornier Do17s. Page had managed to bale out of his aircraft into the Channel but he had suffered severe burns and then spent much of the next two years in hospitals undergoing numerous operations and recovering from his injuries. He then returned to operations towards the end of 1942 and had briefly served in North Africa but the extreme heat had caused him further skin problems and so he returned to the UK. Page then converted to the Mustang and was soon adding to his total and during one *Ranger* sortie across France in June 1943 he and his squadron commander shot down six aircraft in just a matter of minutes; Page being credited with two and a half kills. Page was awarded the DFC but his injuries would still require him to return to hospital for more treatment. Nevertheless he would lead No. 132 Squadron at Ford throughout the period of the D-Day operations and he would later go on to command a wing and add a bar to his DFC, for ten victories, and then a DSO for his outstanding leadership.

There were early successes for the Ford pilots and during one raid, on 23 April, four Mustangs of No. 122 Squadron shot down six Heinkel He111s. The Mustangs were then fitted with bombs and conducted fighter-bomber raids on targets such as railway marshalling yards in northern France. The Mustangs left Ford in mid-May to commence operations from the advanced landing ground at nearby Funtington, swapping places with the Spitfires of No. 144 Wing, which consisted of three Canadian squadrons – Nos 441, 442 and 443 Squadrons.

This newly formed Canadian Wing was led by its wing leader and legendary fighter ace, Wing Commander Johnnie Johnson, who had taken over command just a matter of a few weeks earlier. Born in Leicestershire, the twenty-nine-year-old ace had first achieved success in 1941 while serving with No. 616 Squadron. In 1943 he had commanded the Kenley Wing, after which he had commanded No. 127 Wing following the formation of the 2nd TAF. By the time he arrived at Ford in command of No. 144 Wing, Johnson had been credited with at least twenty-four kills, all fighters, for which he had been awarded the DSO and bar and DFC and bar. Johnson would be the most famous fighter pilot to serve at Ford during the D-Day operations, although he would not add any more kills to his personal total during the month that he flew from the airfield. He would, however, add a second bar to his DSO for his leadership during this period and he would end the war with at least thirty-four kills and had shared in the destruction of at least seven more plus many more claimed as 'probables'.

The Spitfire IX squadrons spent the next three weeks flying a mix of operations across the Channel ranging from fighter raids and bomber escort to low-level fighter-bomber raids against airfields, railway junctions and enemy radar installations in preparation for the Allied invasion of Europe. On D-Day itself all the Ford squadrons flew patrols over the beachhead and invasion area. During the afternoon, a Spitfire of No. 441 Squadron was shot down by flak, although the pilot baled out over the Channel and was saved; somewhat remarkably, this was to be the only Spitfire loss of the day.

During the late morning of the following day, 7 June, one of the flight commanders of No. 443 Squadron, Flight Lieutenant Ian Maclennan, was hit by ground fire while providing air cover over the invasion beaches. Maclennan, a veteran of the Malta campaign with No. 1435 Squadron, for which he was awarded a DFM, and with seven confirmed kills, managed to crash-land on a beach but was captured and spent the next year as a prisoner of war.

The Canadians of No. 144 Wing flew their third patrol of the day over the beachhead during the late afternoon. During their patrol the Spitfires encountered four Focke-Wulf FW190s to the east of Caen. Two pilots of No. 443 Squadron shot down one to the north of Caen and one of the successful pilots sharing the kill was twenty-one-year-old Flying Officer Gordon Ockenden from Alberta; it was his first success of the war and during the next

Ford was home to the Royal Navy's first jet squadron during the 1950s and this Hawker Hunter can be found on Ford Road.

three months he would shoot down four more enemy aircraft for which he would be awarded a DFC. The other successful pilot was Flight Lieutenant Hugh Russell but, sadly, Russell would be shot down and killed not long afterwards during a fighter sweep near Caen during the evening of 16 June; Hugh Russell was just twenty-one years old.

The weather then deteriorated on 9 June, which resulted in a significant reduction in Allied sorties flown and at times brought air operations to a halt. However, once the weather improved, No. 144 Wing then continued its operations as the Allies secured a foothold in Europe with more and more sorties flown on ground attack missions in support of the advancing troops.

The Mosquitos of No. 456 Squadron were also involved in the Allied landings, taking part in nightly patrols over the Channel and northern France. On the night after the D-Day landings the squadron claimed four Heinkel He177s shot down in one engagement and this success was followed by three more enemy aircraft claimed the following night. When the Germans launched the V-1 rocket attacks against London the squadron also took part in the anti-Diver patrols over southern England as more high-speed fighters were used in an attempt to shoot down as many V-1s as possible. The squadron was then joined at Ford by No. 96 Squadron, also equipped with the Mosquito XIII, which enjoyed considerable success having destroyed nearly fifty V-1s in the first few weeks.

Another notable pilot to fly from Ford during this period was Squadron Leader Wally McLeod, the commanding officer of No. 443 Squadron. Born in Canada in 1915, McLeod had joined the RCAF in 1940 and moved to the UK the following year. He made his name in the Middle East and then Malta while flying Spitfires with No. 603 Squadron and then No. 1435 Squadron, during which time he became one of the top-scoring aces in Malta for which he was awarded a DFC and bar. By the time he was given command of No. 443 Squadron in February 1944 he had been credited with at least thirteen confirmed kills and there were probably many more that could not be confirmed but are likely to have ended up in the sea off Malta. During the late evening of 14 June, while escorting more than 200 Lancasters of Bomber Command in a raid on the port of Le Havre, McLeod added another kill to his total when he shot down a Dornier

Do217 to the south-west of Le Havre. During the next few weeks, Wally McLeod added to his total making him, at the time, the RCAF's top-scoring ace of the war with at least twenty-one confirmed kills, for which he added a DSO to his awards. Sadly, however, he did not see out the campaign and was last seen engaging several Messerschmitt Bf109s over Nijmegen on 27 September but he failed to return from the sortie. His body was not found until after the war, when it was discovered still in the wreckage of his aircraft; Wally McLeod is buried in the Rheinberg war cemetery.

Spitfires of No. 453 Squadron were the first aircraft from Ford to operate from hastily prepared airstrips in Normandy having landed in France just four days after the invasion had taken place but it was the Canadians of No. 144 Wing that were the first to move across the Channel when they left Ford for St Croix-sur-Mer (B.3) on 15 June. On the same day the Spitfires of No. 602 Squadron also crossed the Channel to operate from St Croix-sur-Mer but they returned to Ford later in the day.

The following evening No. 144 Wing, led by Johnnie Johnson, was joined by the Australians of No. 453 Squadron from Ford, led by Squadron Leader Don Smith, on a fighter sweep over the Caen area. The twelve Spitfires of No. 453 Squadron spotted several Messerschmitt Bf109s below them and immediately attacked. During the following minutes the squadron shot down two of the Bf109s and claimed a further three as damaged; none of its Spitfires were lost. However, tragedy then struck.

Looking to the north-east along the main runway with the entrance to Ford Airfield Market on the right.

The Spitfires of No. 144 Wing had continued the sweep and soon after were bounced by a formation of Focke-Wulf FW190s and during the combat four Spitfires were shot down with the loss of three pilots killed: Squadron Leader James Hall, the commanding officer of No. 442 Squadron, together with Flight Lieutenant Hugh Russell and Flying Officer Luis Perez Gomez of No. 442 Squadron.

Ford then suffered a further devastating loss during a patrol by six Mustangs of No. 122 Squadron during the early evening of 17 June when the squadron's commanding officer, Squadron Leader 'Nipper' Joyce, was shot down and killed. The Mustangs had been jumped by Messerschmitt Bf109s while strafing a train to the south of Evreux. Joyce, just twenty-four years old at the time of his death, was from New Zealand and was a veteran ace of the Western Desert campaign, during which he had been awarded a DFM as a flight sergeant pilot. It was a devastating loss for the squadron. Minutes later, a second section of Mustangs from the squadron was in the area and bombing a railway station at Bourg Achard. The Mustangs then encountered two more Bf109s to the south of Dreux; both Bf109s were shot down without loss. Command of No. 122 Squadron was now given to Squadron Leader John Shaw, another veteran of the Western Desert, where he had commanded No. 32 Squadron. Shaw had risen from the rank of sergeant to squadron leader in a short period of time and he had already been awarded a DSO and a DFC.

During the afternoon of 18 June the Spitfires of No. 132 Squadron, led by Geoffrey Page, were on patrol over the Evreux area when they encountered six Focke-Wulf FW190s. One of the FW190s was claimed as damaged by Page but during the combat the squadron lost one of its aircraft with the loss of Flight Lieutenant Robert Day, a former Defiant night-fighter pilot.

Completely unexpectedly, a strong gale blew up in the Channel during the early hours of 19 June, which brought daylight operations to a standstill for the following three days. The Mustangs of No. 19 Squadron did manage to get airborne during the late afternoon on 20 June to carry out a bombing raid against the railway marshalling yards at Rambouillet. Before the Mustangs reached the target their pilots spotted a number of

Focke-Wulf FW190s and engaged them immediately, shooting down two FW190s and damaging several more. One of the successful pilots was the commanding officer, Squadron Leader 'Mac' Gilmour, who shot down a FW190 over Dreux; it was Gilmour's eighth kill of the war.

The following evening the Mustangs of No. 19 Squadron were over Normandy again, taking part in an armed-reconnaissance sortie to the south of Argentan, when they encountered a dozen Messerschmitt Bf109s; four Bf109s were shot down without loss to the squadron. One of the successful pilots was Flight Lieutenant Deryck Lamb who was quickly making a name for himself at Ford. It was Lamb's fourth success that month for which he would soon receive the DFC. Another pilot to gain success during the encounter that day was Flight Sergeant Basilios Vassiliades of Greek parentage who had joined the RAF in 1941. His success on 21 June was his second but he would go on to be credited with eight kills and awarded the DFM. Sadly, however, Vassiliades would not survive the war; he was killed at the end of March 1945.

Geoffrey Page added to his personal total while leading a patrol of Spitfires from Nos 132 and 602 Squadrons over the eastern beaches during the morning of 22 June, when the patrol encountered more than a dozen enemy aircraft, which resulted in Page shooting down a Focke-Wulf FW190 to the east of Caen.

Leading No. 122 Wing during this period was Wing Commander 'Robin' Johnston. Born in South Africa, Johnston was educated in England and had joined the RAFVR before the outbreak of war. He had made a name for himself while serving with No. 73 Squadron in North Africa and by the time he returned to the UK in early 1944 he had been credited with at least four confirmed kills and had been awarded the DFC. He was then given command of No. 65 Squadron before he was promoted and given command of No. 122 Wing in March. Johnston added to his score during an early morning armed reconnaissance sortie on 24 June when the wing encountered Focke-Wulf FW190s to the south-east of Dreux. His success, a FW190, was his eighth and he would add two more Bf109s to his total by the end of June. By the end of the year he would add a bar to his DFC and a DSO to his awards.

*Twenty-two-year-old Flying Officer
Thorstein Jonsson served at Ford
with No. 65 Squadron during June
1944. The only Icelandic fighter
pilot to serve with the RAF, Jonsson
shot down two Focke-Wulf FW190s
on 24 June, which brought his
personal total to six kills.*

To help illustrate the number of nations that were involved in
the fight against Nazi Germany, one pilot based at Ford during
this period was Flying Officer Thorstein Jonsson of No. 65
Squadron. Known to his colleagues simply as 'Tony', Jonsson
was the only Icelandic fighter pilot to serve with the RAF and
he claimed two victories while flying from Ford during the early
morning of 24 June; two Focke-Wulf FW190s to the south-east of
Dreux, which brought his total to six kills.

No. 65 Squadron provides a good example of a squadron
made up of pilots from different nationalities. Leading the
squadron was Squadron Leader 'Jerry' Westenra, a New
Zealander, who had transferred to the RAF at the end of 1940.
Westenra had already flown a number of different types. First,
Gladiators with No. 112 Squadron in Greece during which time
he had shot down two enemy aircraft, after which he had gone
on to fly Tomahawks, Kittyhawks and Spitfires in North Africa,
claiming more successes and a well earned DFC along the way,
and he was now flying Mustangs. Remarkably, he had achieved
successes flying all five types and he would soon add a bar to
his DFC. Among the other pilots also serving on the squadron

during this period at Ford were another New Zealander, an Australian, four Canadians, a Norwegian and, of course, the Icelander Jonsson.

No. 122 Wing crossed the Channel to take up their new temporary home in France on 25 June. The ground crew had already left earlier for what proved to be a difficult journey. Once the Mustangs had landed at Martragny (B.7) the first responsibility of the pilots was to supervise the re-fuelling and re-arming of their aircraft, making use of whatever camouflage and protection that was available. Then the pilots had to debrief their mission in the army liaison caravan and to be brought up to date with the position of the 'bomb line'. With those essential tasks out of the way the pilots could then get something to eat and find somewhere to get some rest and, if possible, to grab some sleep; this was often in a slit trench close to their aircraft. The squadrons were little over a mile or so from the German lines and once darkness fell, the Germans started shelling the airfield. By day break it was apparent just how much damage had been caused with several aircraft destroyed and three of the ground crew killed. The field hospital had also been hit and three of the nurses were killed. It had not been a good start and for the pilots it was often unnerving to be so close to the front line and to experience war on the ground.

All three squadrons of No. 125 Wing also left Ford on 25 June; No. 132 Squadron moved to Amblie (B.14) with Nos 453 and 602 Squadrons moving to Longues (B.11). The Spitfires were replaced at Ford by the Mustangs of No. 133 Wing, No. 84 Group, which arrived from Holmsley South the following day. The wing consisted of Nos 129, 306 and 315 Squadrons and immediately commenced armed reconnaissance sorties over the Normandy area. Due to losses the wing only stayed at Ford for two weeks before moving to Brenzett in Kent to join the anti-Diver patrols to counter the V-1 rocket threat to London.

A few days later Spitfires of No. 131 Wing, consisting of three Polish squadrons, moved into Ford. The three squadrons were Nos 302, 308 and 317 Squadrons, which moved to Ford before crossing the Channel to operate from Plumetot (B.10). Then, after another few days of inactivity, No. 132 Wing, consisting of four squadrons of Spitfire IXs, moved to Ford. These four squadrons were Nos 66, 127, 331 and 332 Squadrons but, like

The Ford Airfield Commemorative Garden can be found on the corner of Rollaston Park and the B2233 Burndell Road, which runs along the south-western part of the former airfield.

many of the 2nd TAF squadrons, they also moved across the Channel soon after; in the case of No. 132 Wing they moved to Villons les Buissons (B.16).

With the Spitfires gone all that remained at Ford from late August were the Mosquitos of Nos 96 and 456 Squadrons, although the following month No. 96 Squadron moved to Odiham. This triggered the return to Ford of No. 746 Squadron and the Fighter Interception Unit returned to form a Night Fighter Development Wing consisting mainly of Mosquitos and Beaufighters. No. 456 Squadron did enjoy some success against Heinkel He111s used for launching V-1s from the air before the squadron left at the end of the year, leaving only the Night Fighter Development Wing at Ford in early 1945.

After the war Ford was transferred back to the Admiralty and re-commissioned as HMS *Peregrine* once more. The airfield then underwent a major refurbishment programme and, as Royal Naval Air Station Ford, was home to the Royal Navy's first jet squadron during the early 1950s. In 1958 the airfield was closed and the land was transferred to the Home Office for development as an open prison, which opened in 1960, although flying did continue to take place from part of the site for another twenty years. Ford is now a Category D training establishment surrounded by a high security fence with a barrier at the main gate. The site of the former airfield is also used for the Ford Airfield Market and the Flying Fortress Family Fun Centre, as well as many other industrial units located on the Ford Airfield Industrial Estate.

It is easy to find the site of the former airfield and is well worth a visit. From the A27 Chichester to Worthing road at Arundel take the Ford Road southwards towards the village. After crossing the railway line you will enter the village of Ford and this marks the north-east corner of the former airfield. The main runway, which ran south-west to north-east, extended as far as a hundred yards or so from the south of the village. As you continue southwards towards the village of Climping you will see a Hawker Hunter mounted high above the entrance to Ford Airfield Market. Turn right here and the road takes you down to the runway and Ford Airfield Market is on the left. This is accessible to the public and you can drive down the former runway right into the centre of the former airfield.

By returning back to the Ford Road, turn right and continue southwards towards the village of Climping and you are now travelling along the eastern boundary of the former airfield. You will see the former airfield buildings on your right and then pass the entrance to the prison on your left. Then turn right down a minor road, Horsemere Green Lane, to meet the B2233 Yapton Road; if you miss the minor road then just turn right at the T-junction along the A259, which also meets the Yapton Road. Turn right along the Yapton Road north-westwards towards the village of Yapton. After about half a mile you will see a turn to the right called Rollaston Park and on the corner of that junction is the Ford Airfield Commemorative Garden, which came into being in 1989 as a result of work done by local citizens supported by funding from the local government and parishes as well as the Fleet Air Arm Officers Association, and generous donations from local businesses and individuals. This also marks the area where companies operated between the wars when Ford was a civilian airfield. By following the road into Rollaston Park and to the industrial estate you are now travelling along the perimeter track at the north-western part of the former airfield and the extremity of the secondary runway that ran to the south-east.

Squadron	Dates at Ford	Aircraft type
256 Squadron	24 Apr–25 Aug 43	Mosquito XII
418 Squadron RCAF	14 Mar–8 Apr 43	Mosquito II
29 Squadron	3 Sep 43–29 Feb 44	Mosquito XII/ XIII
456 Squadron RAAF	29 Feb–30 Dec 44	Mosquito XVII
19 Squadron	15 Apr–12 May 44	Mustang III
65 Squadron	15 Apr–14 May 44	Mustang III
122 Squadron	15 Apr–14 May 44	Mustang III
132 Squadron	18 Apr–25 Jun 44	Spitfire IX
453 Squadron RAAF	18 Apr–25 Jun 44	Spitfire IX
602 Squadron	18 Apr–25 Jun 44	Spitfire IX
441 Squadron RCAF	14 May–15 Jun 44	Spitfire IX
442 Squadron RCAF	14 May–15 Jun 44	Spitfire IX
443 Squadron RCAF	14 May–15 Jun 44	Spitfire IX
96 Squadron	20 Jun–24 Sep 44	Mosquito XIII
19 Squadron	15–25 Jun 44	Mustang III
65 Squadron	15–25 Jun 44	Mustang III
122 Squadron	15–25 Jun 44	Mustang III
306 'Torunski' Squadron	27 Jun–9 Jul 44	Mustang III
315 'Deblinski' Squadron	26 Jun–10 Jul 44	Mustang III
302 'Poznanski' Squadron	16 Jul–3 Aug 44	Spitfire IX
308 'Krakowski' Squadron	16 Jul–3 Aug 44	Spitfire IX
317 'Wilenski' Squadron	16 Jul–3 Aug 44	Spitfire IX
66 Squadron	12–20 Aug 44	Spitfire IX
127 Squadron	12–20 Aug 44	Spitfire IX
331 (Norwegian) Squadron	12–20 Aug 44	Spitfire IX
332 (Norwegian) Squadron	12–20 Aug 44	Spitfire IX

Funtington

Although its history as an airfield was short-lived, Funtington was amongst the busiest and most successful of the advanced landing grounds used by the 2nd TAF during the period of

D-Day operations. In the space of just five months during 1944 three different types of fighter aircraft – the Typhoon, Mustang and Spitfire – from twenty-four different squadrons, operated from Funtington and the airfield became home to many different nationalities including Canadians, Free French, New Zealanders, Belgians and Norwegians.

The village of Funtington, one of the larger villages in West Sussex, is located some 5 miles to the west of Chichester, on the southern edge of the beautiful South Downs, and midway between Chichester and Havant. It is an extremely pleasant rural parish and the community today is spread over the villages of Funtington, East and West Ashling and West Stoke. The former airfield was situated just off the B2146, which runs northwards to the town of Petersfield.

The site had been identified for development as an advanced landing ground during the summer of 1942 and work began in early 1943, which included the laying of the standard Sommerfeld track runways; the main runway was 1,600 yards long and ran from east to west and the secondary runway of 1,200 yards ran from the south-east to the north-west. Conditions at Funtington, just like most other advanced landing grounds at the time, were basic with accommodation being in tents and the lack of hangars and technical buildings meant that the aircraft had to be serviced and maintained out in the open.

In September 1943 No. 130 Airfield, consisting of two fighter-reconnaissance Mustang squadrons, Nos 4 and 268 Squadrons,

A Typhoon of No. 143 Airfield at Funtington during April 1944.

moved in to Funtington having spent the previous month at Odiham. The squadrons carried out reconnaissance sorties along the French coast and over northern France, occasionally coming into contact with the Luftwaffe, but their stay at Funtington was short-lived and having proved that everything worked the Mustangs moved back to Odiham just three weeks later.

As with other landing grounds, work took place during the winter months to improve the facilities at Funtington; this included the construction of four Blister hangars and hardstandings, and a taxiway to link the dispersals with the runways. By the beginning of April 1944 the airfield was ready for use by the 2nd TAF and within two days the Canadian Typhoon fighter-bomber units of No. 143 Airfield had arrived from Hurn. The Typhoon squadrons carried out fighter-bomber sweeps over northern France, including attacks against key enemy installations, such as radar stations, V-1 flying bomb sites and communications targets, in preparation for the forthcoming Allied invasion of Europe.

No. 143 Airfield was led by the Canadian Wing Commander Bob Davidson who had joined the RAF before the outbreak of war. Davidson had served in the Middle East, Greece and the Western Desert flying Blenheims and Hurricanes with No. 30 Squadron. He had been awarded the DFC for shooting down four enemy aircraft before he returned to the UK where he joined No. 143 Airfield in January 1944 and within days he had scored his first success flying the Typhoon.

The Canadian Typhoon squadrons did not stay for long and very soon moved back to Hurn; they were replaced three days later by the Canadian Spitfire IX squadrons of No. 144 Airfield, which arrived from Westhampnett. While one of the squadrons, No. 442 Squadron, moved almost immediately to Hutton Cranswick to take part in air-to-air gunnery training, the other two squadrons, Nos 441 and 443 Squadrons, immediately set about flying fighter sweep and bomber escort missions over northern France. The squadrons were led by the legendary fighter ace Wing Commander Johnnie Johnson and during one fighter sweep in support of American bombers the Spitfires from Funtington claimed six enemy FW190s destroyed.

Johnson then led the units of No. 144 Airfield on a fighter sweep across the Channel during the early morning of 5 May.

The Spitfires were providing protection for a medium bomber raid against targets in the Lille area and during the sweep they first encountered a formation of Focke-Wulf FW190s near Douai and then forty minutes later they encountered more FW190s near Mons. During the two aerial combats that took place, Johnson first shot down one of the FW190s and during the second engagement three more FW190s were shot down; two were shot down by pilots of No. 441 Squadron and one by Squadron Leader Wally McLeod of No. 443 Squadron. Sadly, one of the Spitfires, flown by Pilot Officer Percy McLachlan, was shot down and the pilot killed.

The following evening there was a further loss for Funtington when Flying Officer Eric Germain of No. 19 Squadron was shot down and killed during a *Ranger* sortie over Denmark. Funtington had sent four Mustangs on the sortie – two each from Nos 19 and 122 Squadrons – and Germain was killed after his formation had been bounced by Focke-Wulf FW190s to the north-east of Aalborg. There had, however, been some success during the sortie when Flight Lieutenant Lance Burra-Robinson of No. 122 Squadron had destroyed a Heinkel Hs 129 on the ground at the airfield of Aalborg; his third success of the campaign.

Commanding No. 441 Squadron during the squadron's early days at Funtington was the Canadian ace Squadron Leader George Hill. Hill had arrived in the UK in early 1942 and had served with Nos 421, 453 and 403 Squadrons before he joined No. 111 Squadron as a flight commander. It was with this squadron that Hill enjoyed so much success and by the time he took command of No. 441 Squadron in March 1944 he had been credited with at least ten confirmed kills and several more shared for which he had been awarded the DFC and two bars. However, his war was to come to an end on 25 April, just two days after he arrived at Funtington, when during a sortie across the Channel in the area of Laon, after sharing in the destruction of a Focke-Wulf FW190, he was shot down. Hill managed to force-land his Spitfire and made his escape but he was later captured and taken as a prisoner of war.

With the return of No. 442 Squadron from Hutton Cranswick, the three squadrons flew a variety of sorties over the Channel – including *Rodeos*, *Rangers* and *Ramrods* – before they left

Mustang IIIs of No. 19 Squadron provided close air support from Funtington on D-Day under the command of Squadron Leader 'Mac' Gilmour as part of No. 122 Wing, No. 83 Group.

Funtington for Ford in mid-May. Replacing the Canadian squadrons at Funtington were the fighter-bomber Mustangs of No. 122 Wing, part of No. 83 Group, which arrived from Ford. The three squadrons – Nos 19, 65 and 122 Squadrons – would now remain at Funtington for the vital build-up to the Allied invasion and would serve together across the Channel during D-Day and the immediate days beyond.

The wing was led by Wing Commander 'Robin' Johnston and three days after arriving at Funtington he led a formation of eight Mustangs from Nos 65 and 122 Squadrons on a long-range sortie across the North Sea to Denmark. The Mustangs first deployed in the morning to Coltishall in Norfolk, where the aircraft were re-fuelled, before the pilots took off to cross the North Sea. During the sortie the Mustang pilots enjoyed considerable success in the Aalborg area when they encountered a number of Junkers Ju88s. Johnston and the commanding officer of No. 65 Squadron, Squadron Leader

Jerry Westenra, were both successful, as was one of the flight commanders, Flight Lieutenant 'Buck' Collyns, who each claimed the destruction of a Ju88 and shared another between them. During the sortie the Mustang pilots also shot down two Junkers W34 trainers in the area and then destroyed a couple of Arado floatplanes moored in a nearby fjord before finally destroying a Heinkel He177, a Messerschmitt Bf109 and another Junkers Ju88 before returning home. The Funtington pilots had destroyed a total of thirteen enemy aircraft during the sortie and had claimed several more as damaged. It was a memorable day, tarnished only by the loss of Flight Lieutenant Barrett who had been shot down by a Focke-Wulf FW190 scrambled from an airfield nearby.

The following evening, 18 May, No. 122 Squadron lost its commanding officer, Squadron Leader Tom Drinkwater, when he was shot down by flak in the Tours area. He was replaced by Squadron Leader 'Nipper' Joyce, a New Zealander who had earlier been awarded a DFM for his success in North Africa when serving as a flight sergeant with No. 73 Squadron. Joyce would command the squadron from Funtington throughout the period of the D-Day operations.

No. 19 Squadron and then No. 122 Squadron each spent a week at Southend during May carrying out an air-to-ground Armament Practice Camp. During the latter half of May the Mustangs flew many *Ranger* sorties across the Channel, including raids over Denmark, which they carried out from airfields in East Anglia, and enjoyed much success. Commanding No. 19 Squadron at Funtington during the D-Day period was Squadron Leader 'Mac' Gilmour. Born in Scotland, Gilmour had served as a sergeant pilot with No. 611 Squadron and was awarded a DFM after his third victory. He then served with No. 111 Squadron in North Africa and was awarded a DFC before he returned to the UK and was given command of No. 19 Squadron in May 1944; Gilmour would end the war with nine confirmed kills.

During the D-Day period the Mustangs of No. 122 Wing were continuously in action, often providing close air support for the army in Normandy. They also carried out other operations ranging from providing fighter escort for Coastal Command Beaufighters, which were carrying out anti-U-boat patrols, to carrying out escort for the tugs and gliders as they flew across the Channel to their pre-determined drop zones. During one such evening sortie on D-Day, while escorting gliders and tugs as part of the second wave of airborne troops, the Mustangs of No. 122 Squadron were attacked by Focke-Wulf FW190s around 9.30 p.m. to the north of Caen but the Mustangs successfully saw off the attackers without any loss.

From first light on the morning of 8 June the Mustangs of No. 65 Squadron, led by Jerry Westenra, were operating in the Dreux area when they encountered several Focke-Wulf FW190s. It was just after 6.00 a.m. when the Mustangs attacked, and during the following few minutes they shot down three of the FW190s; one was shot down by Westenra, his eighth kill of the war, and the other two were shot down by the two flight commanders, Flight Lieutenants Sutherland and Milton; none of the Mustangs were lost.

The weather then deteriorated on 9 June, which resulted in a significant reduction in Allied sorties flown and at times brought air operations to a halt. Better weather saw operations resume, although sadly one of the Mustangs of No. 65 Squadron collided with an enemy aircraft he was seen to be attacking and crashed between Caen and Domfront; Flight Lieutenant Tom Anderson was killed.

The Mustangs of No. 122 Wing were heavily involved in operations across the Channel during the day. Operating in two sections of three, they left Funtington at regular intervals with the task to seek out and attack targets of opportunity. During these patrols the Mustangs occasionally encountered enemy fighters and during one mid-morning patrol Flight Lieutenant 'Buck' Collyns, a New Zealander serving with No. 65 Squadron, shot down a Messerschmitt Bf109 to the south of Caen, although during the same encounter one of the Mustangs was shot down by a Bf109 in the same area with the loss of twenty-two-year-old Flying Officer Pat Driscoll. Soon after, six Mustangs of No. 19 Squadron also found themselves in combat with Bf109s about 10 miles to the south of Caen. The result was that Flight Sergeant Carson shot down one of the Bf109s and a further two were claimed as damaged by the section. Then in the evening, six aircraft of No. 65 Squadron carried out a successful bombing attack against an enemy convoy and one Messerschmitt Bf109 was shot down.

During the following days the Mustangs continued to carry out numerous armed reconnaissance patrols as the Allies began to break out of Normandy. The Funtington Mustangs soon became involved in air-to-air combat with the Luftwaffe over the Normandy beachhead and there were successes and losses on both sides. One loss occurred during the early morning on 14 June when a Mustang of No. 19 Squadron was lost during a dive-bombing sortie; the young Australian, Flight Sergeant Don Kairton, was killed. Later that day, six Mustangs of No. 65 Squadron were flying an armed reconnaissance sortie to the south-west of Rouen when they encountered several Messerschmitt Bf109s in the area. During the air combat that followed the Mustangs claimed one Bf109 as destroyed and three more as either probably destroyed or at least damaged. Minutes later, a second section of Mustangs from Funtington, this time from No. 19 Squadron, encountered more Bf109s in the area and claimed two more shot down; no Mustangs were lost during the engagements.

The period of intense operations came to an end during mid-June when the wing moved to Ford for preparation for a move across the Channel and by the end of the month the squadrons were operating from Martragny (B.7). The Mustangs were replaced at Funtington by four squadrons of Typhoons of Nos 123 and 136 Wings, which started to arrive from Thorney Island on 17 June. The squadrons spent the next few days preparing to move across the Channel and within the week had all moved on to Hurn prior to deploying across to France.

The local villagers of Funtington were now used to seeing a high turn over of aircraft and squadrons, and the next units to arrive were the Spitfire IXs of No. 145 'Free French' Wing, part of No. 84 Group, which arrived from Merston on 22 June. No. 329 'Cicognes' Squadron had formed in Scotland earlier in the year on arrival from North Africa where it had been operating with the *Armée de l'Air*. It had then moved to Perranporth, where it took delivery of its Spitfires, initially MkVs and then MkIXs, before the squadron became operational in March and then joined No. 145 Wing at Merston in April. No. 340 'Ile-de-France' Squadron had formed much earlier, in 1941, as a Free French squadron equipped with Spitfires. It had been in the UK ever since and, with the other Free French squadrons of the wing, had provided fighter cover over Normandy during the D-Day landings. No. 341 'Alsace' Squadron had formed in Scotland in 1943 from the Free French Flight, which had been operating in the Western Desert. During 1943 the squadron had conducted fighter sweeps across the Channel from its base at Biggin Hill before the squadron moved to Perranporth and then Merston to join the wing.

For the next two weeks the French squadrons took part in fighter sweeps and bomber escort duties from Funtington but it was also soon time to move on and at the beginning of July the wing moved to Selsey, and then Tangmere, before its personnel had the opportunity to return back to France in August; it would have been a great moment after so many years of waiting. Next to arrive at Funtington on the 'merry-go-round' of squadrons was No. 135 Wing, which arrived from Coolham on 4 July. By comparison with other movements during the summer of 1944, the three squadrons – Nos 222, 349 and 485 Squadrons – were to stay at Funtington for a while and for the next month carried out bomber escort duties for Mitchells and Bostons, as well as some of the heavy bombers of Bomber Command. With No. 349 Squadron being a Belgian squadron and No. 485 Squadron being Royal New Zealand Air Force, it was a mixed wing and it soon increased in size by the addition of a fourth squadron, No. 33 Squadron, which arrived from Tangmere on 17 July.

Leading No. 135 Wing was Wing Commander Ray Harries. Born in South Wales, Harries had achieved success flying Spitfires with No. 131 Squadron and then commanding No. 91 Squadron during 1943, which had been the first unit to receive the new Griffon-powered Spitfire MkXII. His number of victories soon mounted and by the end of 1943 he was the wing leader at Westhampnett and had been awarded a DSO and a DFC and two bars. Harries had then been sent to the United States to lecture on fighter and wing tactics before he returned to the UK in the spring of 1944 to take command of No. 135 Wing. Harries would later be awarded a bar to his DSO and would remain in the post-war RAF only to lose his life in 1950 during an accident while flying a Meteor jet fighter.

It was soon time for No. 135 Wing to move on and it was replaced the same day, 6 August, by No. 132 Wing, also equipped with four squadrons of Spitfire IXs, which arrived from Tangmere. This wing included two Norwegian squadrons – Nos 331 and 332 Squadrons – which meant that in the space of just four months Funtington had been home to Canadians, Free French, New Zealanders, Belgians and Norwegians, as well as the other RAF squadrons. For the next week the four squadrons flew a mix of sorties. In addition to its familiar role of bomber escort, the Spitfires also took part in a number of ground attack missions. Then, just like the other wings before them, it was time for No. 132 Wing to leave Funtington and move to Ford before making the move across the Channel later that month.

The Spitfires of No. 132 Wing were the last aircraft to operate from Funtington and after their departure on 12 August the airfield was empty; the Allied break out of Normandy towards Germany had meant that the battle had now to be fought from elsewhere. Since the arrival of the first Canadian Typhoons just five months earlier it had been non-stop for the personnel at Funtington, during which time the airfield had been home to twenty-four different squadrons. Now, almost without warning, the sky around the village was silent and only the birds could be heard once more. The airfield at Funtington was closed at the end of 1944 and the site was soon cleared before the land reverted back to agriculture, although part of the land has since been used as a research establishment and has been used by QinetiQ, the British global defence and technology company, since 2001.

There is very little of the former airfield to see apart from some bits of the perimeter track and some concrete from hangar bases that were never used. The village of Funtington can be found by taking the B2146 northwards from the A27, and from the village the site of the former airfield can be found by heading westwards along Common Road towards the village of Aldsworth. The road you are travelling along follows the line of the main runway and you will see a pig farm on your left and the QinetiQ site on your right. Continuing along Common Road you will see a public bridleway to your left, which leads down to Jubilee Wood and this marks the area from where the secondary runway once ran to the north-east.

Squadron	Dates at Funtington	Aircraft type
4 Squadron	15 Sep– 6 Oct 43	Mustang I
268 Squadron	15 Sep– 8 Oct 43	Mustang I
438 Squadron RCAF	3– 20 Apr 44	Typhoon I
439 Squadron RCAF	2–19 Apr 44	Typhoon I
440 Squadron RCAF	2–19 Apr 44	Typhoon I
441 Squadron RCAF	23 Apr–14 May 44	Spitfire IX
442 Squadron RCAF	22 Apr–14 May 44	Spitfire IX
443 Squadron RCAF	22 Apr–14 May 44	Spitfire IX
19 Squadron	20 May–15 Jun 44	Mustang III
65 Squadron	14 May–15 Jun 44	Mustang III
122 Squadron	14 May–15 Jun 44	Mustang III
164 Squadron	17–21 Jun 44	Typhoon I
198 Squadron	18–22 Jun 44	Typhoon I
609 Squadron	18–22 Jun 44	Typhoon I
183 Squadron	18–22 Jun 44	Typhoon I
329 (Free French) Squadron	22 Jun–1 Jul 44	Spitfire IX
340 (Free French) Squadron	22 Jun–1 Jul 44	Spitfire IX
341 (Free French) Squadron	22 Jun–1 Jul 44	Spitfire IX
485 Squadron RNZAF	4 Jul–7 Aug 44	Spitfire IX
222 Squadron	4 Jul–6 Aug 44	Spitfire IX
349 (Belgian) Squadron	4 Jul–6 Aug 44	Spitfire IX
33 Squadron	17 Jul–6 Aug 44	Spitfire IX
66 Squadron	6–12 Aug 44	Spitfire IX
127 Squadron	6–12 Aug 44	Spitfire IX
331 (Norwegian) Squadron	6–12 Aug 44	Spitfire IX
332 (Norwegian) Squadron	6–12 Aug 44	Spitfire IX

Merston

Less than 2 miles to the south-east of Chichester, and just to the south of the A259 road to Bognor Regis, is the village of Merston and during the period of D-Day operations its airfield was home to three 'Free French' Spitfire squadrons of the RAF.

Looking westwards along Common Road towards the village of Aldsworth, with the QinetiQ site to the right and a pig farm to the left, which marks the line of the former main runway at Funtington.

The airfield was identified just before the start of the Second World War as a suitable satellite for nearby Tangmere, just 3 miles away and one of Fighter Command's main operating airfields, when it looked like hostilities were inevitable. It was some time before the airfield at Merston was ready for use and it was not used during the Battle of Britain; the airfield was grass, and some buildings had been erected around its perimeter, but the ground became waterlogged whenever it rained.

With Britain having fought off the threat of invasion, at least for the time being, work continued on the site during the latter months of 1940, including the construction of six hangars and fighter dispersals with blast pens, and the airfield finally opened during the following spring. It was initially only ever intended that Merston would accommodate just one of Tangmere's fighter squadrons at any one time and the first squadron of Spitfires from the Tangmere wing moved in during May 1941. The waterlogged site and poor drainage caused problems during the autumn and winter months of 1941 because there was little activity from the airfield until the spring of 1942 when activity increased during the summer with the arrival of a second squadron.

At the end of the summer the two RAF squadrons moved back to Tangmere and American fighter squadrons moved in. The drainage continued to be a problem and the Americans moved out later in the year after which an airfield construction unit moved in to improve the site. During the winter of 1942–43 two Sommerfeld tracks were laid as runways, with the main runway of approximately 1,500 yards in length running in a south-west to north-east direction. More accommodation was built and a number of aircraft hardstandings were constructed with the work being completed by May 1943 when Merston was re-opened.

The airfield and facilities were now sufficient to allow two squadrons to operate together. The first aircraft to arrive were Spitfire Vs of No. 485 Squadron, which arrived from Westhampnett on 21 May, followed a week later by the arrival of Hurricane IV rocket-armed fighter-bombers of No. 184 Squadron from Eastchurch. The Hurricanes did not stay long and they were soon replaced by Typhoons of No. 174 Squadron, which, in turn, left Merston just two weeks later. Following a short detachment to Scotland, No. 485 Squadron then left Merston at the end of June and moved to Biggin Hill; Merston had been active for less than six weeks.

During mid-August, two Canadian Spitfire V squadrons – Nos 402 and 416 Squadrons – moved south from Digby to take

Typhoons of No. 181 Squadron arrived at Merston at the end of 1943 and remained at the airfield until April 1944 when they moved to Hurn.

part in fighter sweeps and escort, as well as some ground-attack missions over France. As there was sufficient space at Merston the squadrons were soon joined by a third squadron, No. 118 Squadron, also equipped with Spitfire Vs, which arrived from Westhampnett.

By the middle of September the squadrons had left Merston and the airfield was prepared for the arrival of the 2nd TAF units in preparation for the forthcoming Allied invasion of Europe. The first Typhoon wing – consisting of Nos 181, 182 and 247 Squadrons – began arriving at Merston on 8 October and the build-up was complete just a few days later. With the exception of a few short periods when the squadrons were detached away, these three Typhoon squadrons would remain at Merston until the end of March 1944.

The Merston wing then became No. 124 Airfield, part of No. 83 Group, led by Wing Commander B G Carroll with the Norwegian Wing Commander Erik Haabjörn as Wing Commander Flying. The Typhoons took part in a variety of sorties, including fighter sweeps and bomber escort, attacks against enemy shipping and attacks against V-1 sites. More air-to-ground offensive operations continued over northern France during early 1944 before the squadrons converted to a rocket-firing capability, specifically against troop compounds and communications targets.

At the beginning of April No. 124 Airfield moved to Hurn and was replaced by the Spitfires of No. 145 'Free French' Airfield, which arrived from Perranporth, and it would be these three French squadrons – Nos 329, 340 and 341 Squadrons – that would operate from Merston during the period of D-Day operations. The squadrons were initially tasked to carry out fighter sweeps over northern France but the Spitfires were soon modified with bomb racks and following a short period of training at Llanbedr, lasting just a few days, the squadrons began dive-bombing operations.

Leading the French wing was twenty-eight-year-old Wing Commander Bill Crawford-Compton. Born in New Zealand, Crawford-Compton had found his way to the UK where he joined the RAF as a sergeant pilot soon after the outbreak of war. Commissioned in 1941 he flew Spitfires with No. 485 Squadron RNZAF, during which he shot down six enemy aircraft and was awarded a DFC, before he joined No. 611 Squadron as a flight

Spitfire IXs of No. 340 Squadron operated from Merston as part of the Free French Wing during the D-Day operations.

commander in August 1942. Having claimed more successes, for which he had earned a bar to his DFC, Crawford-Compton was given command of No. 64 Squadron and then the Hornchurch Wing. By the time he arrived at Merston to assume command of No. 145 Wing, Crawford-Compton had been credited with at least sixteen confirmed kills for which he had added a DSO to his awards. Crawford-Compton would add a further three kills to his total before he handed over command of No. 145 Wing and would add a bar to his DSO for his outstanding leadership during the period of the Normandy landings and in the weeks beyond. Bill Crawford-Compton would later remain in the post-war RAF and reach the rank of air vice-marshal.

On D-Day the Merston wing flew low-level fighter cover over the Allied ships and beachhead and the following day enjoyed some success during an engagement with the Luftwaffe to the north of Caen when Bill Crawford-Compton shot down a Junkers Ju88 to the west of Caen during a morning engagement that saw eight other Ju88s shot down by the Canadian No. 126 Wing from Tangmere.

The weather then deteriorated on 9 June, which resulted in a significant reduction in Allied sorties flown and at times brought air operations to a halt. Better weather saw operations resume and No. 145 Wing was soon in action over Normandy the following day. During the afternoon one of the Spitfires had to make a forced landing at one of the emergency landing strips after it had been damaged. The pilot was Wing Commander David Scott-Malden who was serving as a staff officer in No. 84

Group at the time but had voluntarily flown with the wing that afternoon. Born in Sussex, Scott-Malden had achieved a number of successes flying Spitfires with No. 603 Squadron and later when leading the North Weald wing during 1942, receiving a DFC and bar. Since then he had held a number of appointments, including being the liaison officer to the US Eighth Air Force, after which he became the wing leader of the Hornchurch wing from October 1943 until February 1944. He had also added a DSO to his awards and would later be given command of No. 125 Wing in France after the Allied invasion; Scott-Malden would remain in the post-war RAF, eventually reaching the rank of air vice-marshal.

One of the most interesting characters who flew from Merston during this period was the twenty-three-year-old Frenchman, Denys Boudard, who, along with a friend, had escaped from France in 1941 in a stolen German training aircraft with both men dressed as German aircraft mechanics. Sadly, his colleague was later killed but Boudard survived his time at Merston and would later fly the first Allied aircraft into Carpiquet.

A strong gale blew up in the Channel during the early hours of 19 June, which brought daylight operations to a standstill for the following three days. With the improvement in weather, the Merston wing maintained its support of the Allied invasion and on 22 June moved to nearby Funtington as part of a general rotation of fighter wings around the southern airfields and landing grounds.

The Free French wing of the 2nd TAF was replaced at Merston by Spitfires of the ADGB, which had been tasked to reinforce the fighter squadrons preparing to move across the Channel to support the Allied advance towards Germany, but their stay at Merston lasted just a few days and No. 142 Wing moved in to Merston from Westhampnett at the end of June. Equipped with Spitfire Vs, the squadrons spent their six weeks at Merston mainly flying bomber escort sorties for the light-medium bombers of No. 2 Group and were the last operational aircraft to fly from Merston during the war.

By mid-August the wing had gone and by the end of the Second World War the airfield's buildings were being used as accommodation for many units that were being disbanded at the end of the war. The airfield was then placed on care and maintenance and after the war Merston was transferred to the Admiralty and for a while much equipment was stored in the hangars and buildings around the site. However, all but a few signs of the former airfield have long gone, although some shelters survived and part of the former perimeter track has been used over the years as a farm road. The main roundabout where the A27 Chichester Ring Road meets the A259 road to Bognor Regis marks the north-western corner of the former airfield. If you travel south-eastwards along the A259 then you will be following a line along the northern boundary of the site; the minor road heading southwards, Vinnetrow Road, marks the western boundary. Following the A259 towards Bognor Regis, after about a mile you will see nurseries on your right, which mark the northern part of the former airfield, and Green Lane, which runs parallel to the south of the main road, is part of the former perimeter track.

Squadron	Dates at Merston	Aircraft type
181 Squadron	8 Oct–31 Dec 43	Typhoon I
182 Squadron	12 Oct–31 Dec 43	Typhoon I
247 Squadron	11 Oct–31 Dec 43	Typhoon I
181 Squadron	13 Jan–6 Feb 44	Typhoon I
182 Squadron	21 Jan–1 Apr 44	Typhoon I
247 Squadron	13 Jan–1 Apr 44	Typhoon I
181 Squadron	21 Feb–1 Apr 44	Typhoon I
329 (Free French) Squadron	17 Apr–22 Jun 44	Spitfire IX
340 (Free French) Squadron	17 Apr–22 Jun 44	Spitfire IX
341 (Free French) Squadron	17 Apr–22 Jun 44	Spitfire IX
80 Squadron	22–27 Jun 44	Spitfire IX
229 Squadron	24–27 Jun 44	Spitfire IX
274 Squadron	22–28 Jun 44	Spitfire IX
130 Squadron	27 Jun–3 Aug 44	Spitfire V
303 Squadron	26 Jun–9 Aug 44	Spitfire V
402 Squadron RCAF	27 Jun–8 Aug 44	Spitfire V

Selsey

The advanced landing ground at Selsey in West Sussex was only in existence for a year during the period 1943–44 but it was home to a wing of Spitfires during the D-Day operations and was one of the most successful of the 2nd TAF's ALGs. But not all landing grounds in Sussex were developed as a result of the survey carried out in 1942 and occasionally a site that had seen activity long before the outbreak of hostilities in Europe was found suitable. The small airfield of Selsey was one such ALG, having previously been used as a private airfield before the Second World War. Unsurprisingly, therefore, in 1942 the grass site located adjacent to the village of Church Norton was identified and surveyed as a potential advanced site for development.

As with many sites identified for potential use as airfields, there was opposition from the Ministry of Agriculture but eventually development of the site commenced towards the end of 1942. Two Sommerfeld track runways, made up of heavy steel netting held rigid, were laid. The main runway was laid in a north-east to south-west direction and was approximately 1,400 yards in length and the second runway, which was 1,300 yards in length, was laid at ninety degrees to the main runway and ran along a south-east to north-west direction. Similar to other ALGs, the temporary facilities at Selsey included metal hardstandings, a perimeter track and two Blister hangars for aircraft maintenance. As far as accommodation was concerned, the facilities at Selsey were better than at other ALGs because a number of local buildings were requisitioned for use whereas at other ALGs the airfield's personnel were usually accommodated in tents.

Work had to be completed by the spring of 1943 and the airfield was ready in time for the first aircraft to arrive. At the end of May 1943 Spitfire Vs of No. 65 Squadron arrived from Fairlop followed by the arrival of Typhoons of No. 245 Squadron, which arrived from the same airfield. The two squadrons formed No. 121 Airfield and nearby Norton Priory used as its headquarters with its grounds used for tents to accommodate many of the squadrons' personnel. However, both squadrons did not remain long. As with other ALGs their presence had tested the capability of Selsey and after a month both squadrons moved to Kent; No. 65 Squadron moved to Kingsnorth and No. 245 Squadron to Lydd.

Improvements were then made to Selsey as preparations were put in place for the arrival of more aircraft in the build-up to the Allied invasion of Europe. Four additional Blister hangars were erected for aircraft maintenance and more metal hardstandings put in place. Development work had to be completed by the spring of 1944 and in early April three squadrons of Spitfire IXs of No. 135 Airfield, No. 84 Group, moved into Selsey from Hornchurch. The first squadron to arrive was No. 485 Squadron RNZAF followed by No. 222 Squadron and then No. 349 (Belgian) Squadron.

Operations commenced soon after, which included fighter sweeps and fighter escort for bombers attacking targets in northern France, and in May the wing was renamed as No. 135 Wing. An example of the type of operations flown during the weeks leading up to D-Day was *Ramrod* 905, which was flown by the Spitfires of No. 222 Squadron on 21 May and involved train-busting in the Somme-Seine area. The squadron was being led by Squadron Leader Innes and the Spitfires proceeded to Friston with 30-gallon tanks where the aircraft were re-fuelled while the pilots carried out their final briefing. Take-off was at 10.30 a.m. and the Spitfires coasted in over Ault at a height of 10,000 feet before the squadron split into three sections. There was a complete cloud layer beneath them and once the Spitfires had descended through the cloud base, which was at 2,500 feet, Blue Section proceeded to the Amiens area, Red Section went to Gournay and Yellow Section went to the Forges area. The Spitfires of Blue Section were fortunate to find some targets and destroyed a locomotive and two trains. Red Section did not find any movement on the railways but instead ran into some flak and Yellow Section destroyed a signal box and some goods wagons; two of Yellow Section's Spitfires were damaged during the attack.

On D-Day the Selsey Spitfires were involved in air patrols over the beaches. Their first success, and indeed the 2nd TAF's first aerial success of D-Day, was during the afternoon when the Spitfires of No. 135 Wing spotted a formation of Junkers Ju88s near Caen and heading towards the invasion fleet. With No. 222 Squadron providing top cover, the Kiwis of No. 485 Squadron attacked first, followed by the Belgians of No. 349 Squadron and in the space of just fifteen minutes the Selsey Spitfires shot down four of the Ju88s and claimed another four as damaged. One of the successful pilots was twenty-one-year-old Flying Officer John Houlton of No. 485 Squadron who shot down two of the Ju88s, although the second was shared with the rest of his section. Born in Christchurch, New Zealand, Houlton had been with the squadron for just over a year having previously served in Malta. The first Ju88 he destroyed on D-Day was later credited as being the Allies' first aerial success of the day.

During the first days after D-Day the Selsey Spitfires occasionally flew as a wing over the invasion area as the Allies began taking a foothold in Europe. In the early morning of 7 June, the Spitfires of No. 349 Squadron were operating to the south-west of Caen when they came into contact with Focke-Wulf FW190s and Flight Lieutenant Seydel claimed one as damaged. Seydel was in action again early the following morning, just after first light, when his squadron was operating with No. 485 Squadron over the invasion area. Several bomb-carrying Focke-Wulf FW190s were spotted to the south of Trouville and during the aerial combat that followed one of the FW190s was shot down by Seydel and his wingman, Warrant Officer Clarke, although the squadron lost one of its Spitfires, flown by Flight Sergeant Gheyssens, to the west of Dinan-sur-Mer; Gheyssens was killed. During the same engagement, another FW190 was shot down by Flying Officer Yeatman just to the south-east of St Aubin.

Early that evening the Selsey Spitfires of No. 135 Wing were in action again, this time providing low-level cover over the area around Caen, when they spotted some thirty or more enemy aircraft – a mix of Focke-Wulf FW190s and Messerschmitt Bf109s – heading for the Allied troops. While No. 349 Squadron provided cover, the Spitfires of Nos 222 and 485 Squadrons attacked. Led by its new commanding officer, twenty-four-years-old Squadron Leader David Cox, a veteran of the Battle of Britain and with a DFC and bar to his name, the Spitfires of No. 222 Squadron shot down three of the FW190s and damaged another, and damaged at least three of the Bf109s, while No. 485 Squadron shot down three Bf109s and a FW190, and damaged a further two FW190s. No Spitfires were lost; it had been a great day for the Selsey wing.

The weather then deteriorated on 9 June, which resulted in a significant reduction in Allied sorties flown and at times brought air operations to a halt. Better weather saw operations resume and the Spitfires of No. 222 Squadron were in action early the following morning over the eastern beaches of the invasion area and Flight Lieutenant Varley shot down a Focke-Wulf FW190. During the same patrol, however, one of the Spitfires had been forced to make an emergency landing on one of the beaches along the coastline; unfortunately, the beach was still in enemy hands and the pilot was taken as a prisoner of war.

That same day, 10 June, a section of No. 349 Squadron landed across the Channel at a prepared landing strip at Bazenville, later designated B.2, to re-fuel and re-arm; therefore becoming the first Allied aircraft known to land across the Channel after D-Day. Three days later aircraft of No. 485 Squadron operated from a strip at St Croix-sur-Mer (B.3) during daylight hours, which enabled them to enjoy a longer time on task over the Normandy area, before returning to Selsey at dusk.

By now Flying Officer Johnny Houlton had added a further Messerschmitt Bf109 to his total, which he had shot down on 12

A plaque on the Selsey Heritage Trail, which can be found on the northern side of Rectory Lane leading down towards Church Norton, marks the site of the former airfield of Selsey.

June to the south-west of Aunay-sur-Odon; his third success of the D-Day period and his fourth of the war for which he would later be awarded the DFC. During that same early morning patrol over the beaches, another Bf109 was shot down by Flight Lieutenant Newenham.

In addition to its fighter duties the Spitfires also carried bombs from mid-June before the three squadrons left Selsey at the end of the month when they moved to Coolham. They were replaced by three more squadrons of Spitfire IXs, No. 145 (French) Wing, which consisted of Nos 329, 340 and 341 Squadrons. The wing was led by Wing Commander Bill Crawford-Compton and by the time he arrived at Selsey in command of No. 145 Wing he had at least nineteen confirmed victories; he added his twentieth victory during a sortie from Selsey on 9 July when he shot down a Messerschmitt Bf109 to the north of Bernay.

The French of No. 145 Wing were briefly joined by No. 74 Squadron during July before the wing moved out from Selsey for Tangmere in early August. Their departure triggered the return to Selsey of No. 135 Wing to carry out bomber escort duties. However, their stay was short-lived and two of the squadrons, Nos 222 and 349 Squadrons, moved to Tangmere while No. 33 Squadron crossed the Channel to operate from the landing strip designated B.10 at Plumetot.

Although the last five months either side of D-Day had been particularly busy for the airfield of Selsey, just like other ALGs its war was over as far as air operations were concerned. By the end of the war the land was already being used by local farmers and following the declaration of peace in Europe the runways, hardstandings and hangars were removed and the land fully reverted to agriculture.

Today there are virtually no signs whatsoever of this former airfield that occupied the open fields at Church Norton to the north of Selsey. A plaque, which is one of a number of blue plaques marking the Selsey Heritage Trail, marks the edge of the former airfield. The plaque can be found on the north side of Rectory Lane, which leads to Church Norton off the B2145 Chichester Road about a mile to the north of Selsey.

Squadron	Dates at Selsey	Aircraft type
65 Squadron	31 May–1 Jul 43	Spitfire V
245 Squadron	1–30 Jun 43	Typhoon I
485 Squadron RNZAF	7 Apr–30 Jun 44	Spitfire IX
222 Squadron	11 Apr–30 Jun 44	Spitfire IX
349 (Belgian) Squadron	11 Apr–30 Jun 44	Spitfire IX
329 (Free French) Squadron	1 Jul–6 Aug 44	Spitfire IX
340 (Free French) Squadron	1 Jul–14 Aug 44	Spitfire IX
341 (Free French) Squadron	1 Jul–6 Aug 44	Spitfire IX
74 Squadron	17–24 Jul 44	Spitfire IX
33 Squadron	6–19 Aug 44	Spitfire IX
222 Squadron	6–19 Aug 44	Spitfire IX
349 (Belgian) Squadron	6–19 Aug 44	Spitfire IX

Tangmere

This is one of the RAF's most famous fighter airfields having been used extensively during the Battle of Britain and then during the period building up to D-Day and beyond; it was one of the busiest airfields of the 2nd TAF. Located about 3 miles to the north-east of Chichester, Tangmere's history dates back to the First World War when in 1917 the 200 acres of land was developed as an airfield following a forced landing of an aircraft on what was then Bayleys Farm. The airfield was used by the British and Americans during the latter period of the First World War and when hostilities were over the airfield was used as a holding station for units returning from France. The airfield then closed in 1920 but the land was retained by the Air Ministry until 1925 when Tangmere re-opened as a Coastal Area unit.

Improvements were made to the facilities at Tangmere during the late 1920s and early 1930s, during which time the airfield was home to Gamecocks and Siskins, and then the Hawker Fury. The RAF's Expansion Scheme during 1936–37 brought further changes to Tangmere as new squadrons arrived. The airfield was extended to the east to provide greater runway length and

Born in America to Canadian parents, Wing Commander George Keefer was given command of No. 126 Wing at Tangmere in April 1944, by which time he had been awarded a DFC and bar. He was still only twenty-two years old when he led the wing on D-Day.

a hardened perimeter track constructed, and there had also been considerable improvement to the buildings and support facilities. New aircraft arrived during the later months of 1938 and at the start of the Second World War Tangmere was home to Hurricanes and Gladiators.

The period of the Phoney War lasted several months and several squadrons moved in and out of Tangmere. During the Battle of Britain Tangmere was the sector airfield for Sector A of No. 11 Group, Fighter Command, and was home to four squadrons of Hurricanes and to the Blenheims of the Fighter Interception Unit. The airfield came under attack in the early afternoon of 16 August, which resulted in the destruction of two hangars with three more seriously damaged. Many of the station's technical and domestic buildings were also destroyed and the station was left without water and sanitation. A number of aircraft that had been caught on the ground had also been damaged and thirteen of the station's personnel, including three civilians, were killed with many more injured. Despite the extensive damage, Tangmere remained operational, although the operations room was moved to a school in Chichester and many of the station's personnel were dispersed.

After the Battle of Britain, Tangmere was used by a number of different aircraft and units. Some of the more interesting residents included Special Duty units used to ferry agents of the Special Operations Executive into occupied France. Throughout

1941–42 several improvements were made to the airfield, including the construction of two asphalt runways; the longest being nearly 2,000 yards in length. These runways often proved most useful for damaged bombers returning from operations over Germany.

By the time that the 2nd TAF had been formed Tangmere was home to Typhoons and Spitfires. Then, as plans materialized for the Allied invasion of Europe, the first Typhoon Wing of No. 84 Group formed at Tangmere at the beginning of February 1944 as No. 146 Airfield. The long-term resident unit, No. 197 Squadron, which had been at Tangmere for nearly a year, was now joined by No. 183 Squadron and No. 257 Squadron. The wing was led by Wing Commander Denys Gillam, a holder of the DSO and DFC and bar, and carried out ground-attack missions across the Channel, specifically against communications targets in northern France. It was also used to seek out and destroy the V-1 flying bomb sites, which were now posing a great threat to southern England.

In March Nos 183 and 197 Squadrons left for Manston and were replaced at Tangmere by Nos 198 and 609 Squadrons, followed a few days later by the arrival of No. 266 Squadron, which moved south from Acklington to join the 2nd TAF. Final preparations were now being made for the Allied invasion of Europe and No. 146 Airfield moved to Needs Oar Point. From mid-April Tangmere then became home to six Canadian squadrons of Nos 126 and 127 Airfields of No. 83 Group, all equipped with Spitfire IXs. First to arrive were Nos 401, 411 and 412 Squadrons from Biggin Hill, followed a few days later by Nos 403, 416 and 421 Squadrons from Kenley. These six Canadian squadrons would remain at Tangmere during the final build-up to D-Day, taking part in a mix of offensive operations, including attacks against V-1 sites and enemy airfields, attacks against enemy communications, as well as bomber escort duties, to help pave the way for the Allied landings.

An example of the success enjoyed by the squadrons during this period was during a fighter escort mission on 7 May when the Spitfires of No. 126 Airfield were escorting American bombers to the Laon area. It was around 9.00 a.m. when the Spitfires encountered a formation of Focke-Wulf FW190s, which had just taken off to intercept the bombers, and during the aerial action that followed, one of No. 411 Squadron's flight commanders, Flight Lieutenant Orr, shot down two of the FW190s to the east of Laon in a matter of minutes. Just behind the Spitfires of No. 126 Airfield, the Spitfires of No. 127 Airfield were providing fighter escort for Bostons of No. 2 Group detailed to attack railway yards when they were bounced by a mixed force of Focke-Wulf FW190s and Messerschmitt Bf 109s; one of the Bf109s was shot down by Flight Lieutenant James Lindsay of No. 403 Squadron and at least two FW190s were damaged.

James Lindsay was to quickly become one of the most successful pilots operating from Tangmere during this period. Born in Ontario, Lindsay had joined the RCAF in 1941 but did not come to the UK until the end of 1943 as he had been retained in Canada as an instructor. No. 403 Squadron was his first operational unit and his success on 7 May had been his first but he would go on to achieve more success over the next few weeks, all against enemy fighters, including the quite staggering achievement of shooting down three Messerschmitt Bf109s in just one minute on 2 July for which he would be awarded a DFC.

The performance and courage of twenty-one-year-old James Lindsay is typical of the young men operating from Tangmere during this period of the war. Three days after Lindsay's first success, on 10 May, No. 126 Airfield was once again operating across the Channel. During the morning the Spitfires were involved in a fighter sweep ahead of a bombing raid by B-26s on railway marshalling yards at Creil, during which the pilots of No. 401 Squadron encountered a formation of Messerschmitt Bf109s, resulting in one of the Spitfires being shot down having probably first destroyed a Bf109, and during the afternoon it was the turn of No. 412 Squadron, led by Squadron Leader Jack Sheppard, which were engaged with Focke-Wulf FW190s to the south of Rheims; the squadron shot down two FW190s for the loss of two pilots, one of which, Flight Lieutenant John Crimmins, was killed.

The success of Jack Sheppard on 10 May was his fourth of the war; all were Focke-Wulf FW190s. The young Canadian had only taken command of the squadron the month before and he would lead the unit throughout the period of the D-Day operations but he would later be shot down by enemy fighters over Normandy on 2 August, although he survived and evaded capture before returning to the UK later in the month.

Despite having more experience than most young pilots experiencing combat for the first time, there were still losses amongst the 2nd TAF's squadron commanders and Tangmere was no exception. An example was when Tangmere suffered a significant loss just a matter of days later when Squadron Leader Norman Fowlow, the commanding officer of No. 411 Squadron, was killed. Born in Newfoundland, Fowlow had joined the RCAF as a sergeant pilot in 1941. Having then been posted to the UK he had served in Malta in 1942 and had then scored success while serving with No. 403 Squadron in the UK the following year. In July 1943 he was posted as a flight commander to No. 421 Squadron having achieved three kills for which he was awarded the DFC. Fowlow had been given command of No. 411 Squadron at Tangmere in April 1944 but during the early evening of 19 May he was carrying out a dive-bombing attack against a railway crossing at Hazebrouck in France when his aircraft was hit by flak, causing the 500lb bomb he was carrying to explode; Norman Fowlow was just twenty-three years old.

The turnover of pilots was quite high as young men were brought into the action and rested as required. The replacements were not all fresh from training and many were experienced veterans of previous campaigns. One example was the young Canadian Flying Officer Harry Fenwick who arrived at Tangmere towards the end of May to join No. 401 Squadron. Fenwick had previously flown Spitfires in North Africa with No. 81 Squadron and had achieved success during the Tunisian campaign where he had been involved in the destruction or damage of many enemy aircraft for which he was awarded the DFC. By the time he arrived at Tangmere he had been personally credited with at least five enemy aircraft with many more either probably destroyed or shared.

On D-Day the Tangmere Spitfires were airborne at Dawn to provide fighter cover over the invasion beaches and during the following critical days they helped provide air cover for the Allied forces as they broke out of Normandy. Throughout this period the wing was led by Wing Commander George Keefer. Born in New York of Canadian parents, Keefer had joined the RCAF in October 1940. After flying Hurricanes in the Middle East with No. 274 Squadron, he returned to the UK and was later given command of No. 412 Squadron before he was awarded a bar to his DFC and given command of No. 126 Wing at Tangmere in April 1944. He was just twenty-two years old when he led the wing over Normandy during the D-Day operations.

During the morning of 7 June, the Spitfires of No. 126 Wing were patrolling the area over Gold beach and towards Caen when they sighted a dozen or more Junkers Ju88s heading for the invasion beaches. The Canadians attacked at once and in the following thirty minutes shot down eight of the Ju88s and claimed damage against a further three. Six of the Ju88s fell to pilots of No. 401 Squadron, including two to the squadron commander, the twenty-two-year-old Canadian ace Squadron Leader Lorne Cameron, his fifth and sixth successes of the war, and one to No. 412 Squadron. One of the Ju88s was shot down by the wing leader, George Keefer; it was his fifth confirmed kill and he would add a sixth success before the end of the day, a Focke-Wulf FW190 over the eastern beaches towards Caen. George Keefer would be rested from operations after the D-Day period but he would return to operational flying before the end of the war and his final score was twelve confirmed kills for which he was also awarded a DSO and bar.

During the early afternoon of 7 June No. 126 Wing flew its second patrol over the beachhead. The Spitfires encountered six Focke-Wulf FW190s to the north-west of Caen and heading towards the invasion area, and so they immediately attacked. During the engagement that followed the Spitfires of No. 401 Squadron shot down one of the FW190s and damaged two more, although one of the Spitfires, flown by Pilot Officer Norman Marshall, was shot down and Marshall was killed. The one squadron success fell to the guns of twenty-one-year-old Flying Officer Bill Klersey from Ontario; his second kill of the war. Klersey would add five more kills to his personal total by the end of July and would finish the war as one of the Canadian's top-scorers with fourteen confirmed victories in the air and having destroyed numerous locomotives and vehicles on the ground for which he was awarded a DSO and a DFC and bar. Sadly, however, during a training exercise immediately

Another young Canadian at Tangmere was Squadron Leader Lorne Cameron who was just twenty-two years old when he commanded No. 401 Squadron during June 1944, scoring two victories on the morning of 7 June and bringing his personal total to six kills for which he was awarded the DFC.

after the war, Bill Klersey crashed his aircraft and was killed; at the time of his death he was still only twenty-two years old.

The wing flew a third patrol of the day in the early evening of 7 June when No. 411 Squadron engaged a number of enemy fighters consisting of Messerschmitt Bf109s and Focke-Wulf FW190s to the north of Caen. The squadron shot down two of the enemy. One was a FW190, which was shot down by the squadron commander, twenty-four-year-old Squadron Leader Graham Robertson, who had assumed command of the squadron just three weeks earlier; his success on 7 June was his first confirmed kill, although he had already claimed a number as probably destroyed or damaged. The second success was a Bf109, which was shot down by Flight Lieutenant George Johnson. Like Robertson, this was his first success of the war and it came the day before his twenty-second birthday. Johnson would go on to be credited with eight confirmed kills, three of them while serving with No. 411 Squadron and the next five with No. 401 Squadron; all eight kills came in the space of three months during the summer of 1944 for which George Johnson was awarded a DFC and bar within a month.

The weather then deteriorated on 9 June, which resulted in a significant reduction in Allied sorties flown and at times brought air operations to a halt. However, once the weather had improved sufficiently operations resumed but during the evening one of the Spitfires of No. 403 Squadron was shot down, possibly by fire from an Allied ship, and came down on Omaha beach, although the pilot escaped with his life and later returned to the UK.

Better weather saw operations resume and the following evening the Spitfires on No. 126 Wing were carrying out a fighter sweep in the Evreux, Chartres and Argentan areas, during which a number of enemy vehicles were spotted and attacked, when they encountered a single Focke-Wulf FW190 and shot it down; the success was shared between Flight Lieutenant Williams of No. 401 Squadron and Flight Lieutenant Nixon of No. 411 Squadron.

In the early morning of 13 June the Spitfires of No. 126 Wing flew across the Channel to the newly prepared landing strip at St Croix-sur-Mer (B.3) and No. 127 Wing deployed to a similar strip prepared at Banville (B.2); the idea was for the Spitfires to fly in at first light and to then carry out operations from across the Channel during the day before returning to Tangmere at Dusk.

That same day, Tangmere suffered a blow when the leader of No. 127 Wing, Wing Commander Lloyd Chadburn, was leading a fighter sweep to the north-east of Caen. Chadburn had been given command of the wing after many notable successes that had seen him awarded a DSO and DFC and bar for his leadership while commanding No. 416 Squadron in 1942, during which time he scored his first success, and then No. 402 Squadron the following year. Chadburn had then become wing leader of the Digby Wing of all-Canadian squadrons in 1943 and by the time he had arrived at Tangmere he had been credited with six personal victories. His loss on 13 June was witnessed by other pilots when, during a patrol over the Normandy beachhead, his aircraft was seen to collide with another Spitfire, flown by Flight Lieutenant Frank Clark of No. 421 Squadron, killing both pilots; Lloyd Chadburn was just twenty-four years old.

Chadburn was immediately replaced by Squadron Leader Bob Buckham, the commanding officer of No. 403 Squadron, who was given command of the wing, and Squadron Leader E P Wood was given command of the squadron. Buckham, another Canadian, was born in British Columbia. His rise from the rank of sergeant pilot to wing commander in little more than two years had been rapid. He had achieved his first aerial success during the Dieppe Raid in August 1942 and by the time he took command of No. 403 Squadron in October 1943 he had been credited with six confirmed kills. Now in command of No. 127 Wing he would lead the wing throughout the remaining period of the D-Day operations.

On 15 June twelve Spitfires of No. 421 Squadron flew to Banville (B.2) to operate from the landing strip during the day before later returning to Tangmere. During an early evening patrol by eight of the squadron's aircraft, the Spitfires encountered a formation of twenty enemy aircraft to the south of Caen. They had encountered a mix of Messerschmitt Bf109s and Focke-Wulf FW190s, and during the air combat that followed the Canadians of No. 421 Squadron shot down seven Bf109s and probably destroyed or at least damaged four more; one of the Spitfires, flown by Flying Officer Lorne Curry, was shot down and the pilot killed.

The squadron's move across the Channel became permanent the following day when No. 127 Wing left Tangmere, followed two days later by the departure of No. 126 Wing, which moved to Beny-sur-Mer (B.4); all three Canadian Spitfire wings were now on the Continent. The following week No. 132 Wing moved in from Bognor, consisting of Nos 66, 331 and 332 Squadrons, and the Czech squadrons (Nos 310, 312 and 313 Squadrons) of No. 134 Wing moved to Tangmere from Appledram. The Czech squadrons soon moved across the Channel and so No. 134 Wing then consisted of Nos 33, 74 and 127 Squadrons, which moved to Tangmere from Lympne.

The Tangmere wings differed in their role with No. 132 Wing providing fighter escort for bombers operating over Europe and No. 134 Wing providing air support for the advancing troops on the ground during the Allied breakout of Normandy. There were further changes in August when both wings moved out and No. 145 Wing, No. 84 Group, consisting of Nos 74, 329, 340 and 341 Squadrons, also equipped with Spitfire IXs, then moved to Tangmere to carry out fighter escort duties. Later in

The Tangmere Military Aviation Museum was founded by a group of enthusiasts and opened in 1982 to help preserve the legacy of this famous wartime airfield.

August the wing moved across the Channel and was replaced by No. 135 Wing, consisting of Nos 222, 349 and 485 Squadrons, but these squadrons only stayed at Tangmere a couple of weeks before crossing the Channel to Carpiquet (B.17) at the end of the month.

After the Second World War the airfield was developed in preparation for the jet age and Tangmere became home to Meteor jet fighters during the 1950s. The airfield was transferred to Signals Command in 1958 and was used by Canberras and Varsities, and was then transferred to Transport Command in 1963 as a non-flying support unit before the airfield closed in 1970. Following the closure of the RAF station, some of the land around the runways was returned to farming. Some of the wartime hangars remained but most of the buildings were demolished during the 1980s as some of the land was used for housing and business. Today the vast majority of the former airfield is now farmed and the runways have been removed, although some of the original RAF buildings remained, including hangars, an accommodation block and the air traffic control tower.

The history of this great airfield has been preserved by the Tangmere Military Aviation Museum, which was founded by a group of enthusiasts and first opened in 1982. The museum contains countless fascinating exhibits. It can be found just to the south of the A27 in Tangmere Road, in one of the original radio repair huts at the edge of the former airfield. The museum is well signposted from the A27 and is maintained by a group of local volunteers. It is open daily from February to November but is closed during December and January. The opening times are: 10.00 a.m. to 4.30 p.m. (February and November) and 10.00 a.m. to 5.30 p.m. (March to October). Admission is £7.50 for adults, £6 for seniors and £2 for children aged 5–16, and children under the age of 5 are free; family admission for two adults and two children is £17. The museum boasts good amenities, including free car parking, a café, souvenir shop and toilets. There is also access for the disabled. The address is: Tangmere Airfield, Chichester, West Sussex PO20 2ES. The telephone number is 01243 790090.

The former air traffic control tower at Tangmere, which has lay derelict for more than forty years, can be found close to the nurseries and to the north-east of the Military Aviation Museum.

From the museum you can clearly see the glasshouses of the nurseries to the east, which mark the area where the middle section of the runway once was. You can walk through the iron gates on to the perimeter track and follow the track northwards, and then continue right, with the three large hangars on your left, for about 200 yards until you see the old air traffic control tower, which is now derelict, just before you reach the nurseries. There are other reminders of the former airfield, such as surviving parts of the perimeter track between the villages of Oving and Aldingbourne to the south and east, and in the village of Tangmere there is the Bader Arms, named after the legendary fighter ace Douglas Bader, and a small memorial stone. The stone can be found near St Andrew's Church, at the junction of Tangmere Road and Church Lane, and was erected by the local population in 1976 to commemorate the airfield. In the church yard there are graves of airmen killed during the Second World War.

Squadron	Dates at Tangmere	Aircraft type
183 Squadron	4 Aug–18 Sep 43	Typhoon I
197 Squadron	28 Mar 43–15 Mar 44	Typhoon I
486 Squadron RNZAF	29 Oct 42–31 Jan 44	Typhoon I
41 Squadron	4 Oct 43–6 Feb 44	Spitfire XII
	20 Feb–11 Mar 44	Spitfire XII
91 Squadron	4 Oct 43–8 Feb 44	Spitfire XII
	20–29 Feb 44	Spitfire XII
183 Squadron	1 Feb–15 Mar 44	Typhoon I
257 Squadron	31 Jan–10 Apr 44	Typhoon I
198 Squadron	17–30 Mar 44	Typhoon I
609 Squadron	16–21 Mar 44	Typhoon I
266 Squadron	22 Mar–10 Apr 44	Typhoon I
197 Squadron	1–10 Apr 44	Typhoon I
401 Squadron RCAF	17 Apr–17 Jun 44	Spitfire IX
411 Squadron RCAF	15 Apr–18 Jun 44	Spitfire IX
412 Squadron RCAF	15 Apr–18 Jun 44	Spitfire IX
403 Squadron RCAF	18 Apr–16 Jun 44	Spitfire IX
416 Squadron RCAF	14 Apr–16 Jun 44	Spitfire IX

Squadron	Dates at Tangmere	Aircraft type
421 Squadron RCAF	18 Apr–16 Jun 44	Spitfire IX
66 Squadron	22 Jun–6 Aug	Spitfire IX
331 (Norwegian) Squadron	22 Jun–6 Aug	Spitfire IX
332 (Norwegian) Squadron	21 Jun–6 Aug	Spitfire IX
310 (Czech) Squadron	22 Jun–3 Jul 44	Spitfire IX
312 (Czech) Squadron	22 Jun–4 Jul 44	Spitfire IX
313 (Czech) Squadron	22 Jun–4 Jul 44	Spitfire IX
33 Squadron	3–17 Jul 44	Spitfire IX
	20–31 Aug 44	Spitfire IX
74 Squadron	3–17 Jul 44	Spitfire IX
127 Squadron	4–12 Jul 44	Spitfire IX
	23 Jul–6 Aug 44	Spitfire IX
74 Squadron	6–19 Aug 44	Spitfire IX
329 (Free French) Squadron	6–19 Aug 44	Spitfire IX
340 (Free French) Squadron	14–19 Aug 44	Spitfire IX
341 (Free French) Squadron	6–19 Aug 44	Spitfire IX
222 Squadron	19–31 Aug 44	Spitfire IX
349 (Belgian) Squadron	19–26 Aug 44	Spitfire IX
485 Squadron RNZAF	19–26 Aug 44	Spitfire IX

Thorney Island

Now the site of Baker Barracks and home to the Royal Artillery, Thorney Island was once home to two Typhoon wings during 1944 and the period of the D-Day operations. Located to the south-east of Havant, and just to the south of Emsworth and the A27 that runs between Portsmouth and Chichester, Thorney Island is a peninsula that juts into Chichester Harbour in West Sussex and is separated from the mainland by a narrow channel called the Great Deep.

The origins of the airfield date back to the mid-1930s when, as part of the RAF's Expansion Scheme, it was decided to build an airfield on the island for Coastal Command. The large site was developed to the east of the road that linked the village of West

A Typhoon of No. 198 Squadron gets airborne from Thorney Island ahead of another mission across the Normandy beaches, June 1944.

Thorney with Emsworth and the airfield was completed at the end of 1937 with six large hangars with concrete hardstandings, and several technical, administrative and domestic buildings all dominating the landscape.

Thorney Island opened as an airfield in February 1938. During the opening months of the Second World War the airfield was extended across and to the south of the Emsworth-West Thorney road, to the point that the airfield completely dominated the island. Thorney Island was used by a number of Coastal Command units during 1940 and, although not a Fighter Command airfield, Thorney Island was still attacked by the Luftwaffe during the height of the Battle of Britain.

During 1941 further improvements began, including the hardening of the runways, with the main runway, which ran from the south-west to the north-east, being extended to 2,000 yards with two shorter runways running from north–south and from the south-east to the north-west. Many squadrons came and went during the following two years but by early 1944 Thorney Island was empty, although the airfield was about to take on a completely new role when it was taken over by the 2nd TAF in preparation for the Allied invasion of Europe.

The first 2nd TAF squadrons to move in to Thorney Island were Nos 164 and 193 Squadrons, equipped with Typhoons,

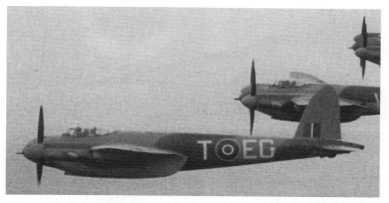

Mosquitos of No. 487 Squadron arrived at Thorney Island when the Typhoons left in mid-June 1944 and stayed at the airfield until February 1945 during which time they mainly carried out intruder missions across north-west Europe.

to form No. 136 Airfield, part of No. 84 Group; these aircraft arrived from Acklington and Fairlop respectively on 15 March. The airfield was commanded by Wing Commander 'Killy' Kilmartin, an Irishman and veteran of the earlier Battles of France and Britain with at least twelve confirmed victories to his name for which he had been awarded the DFC. Prior to arriving at Thorney Island, Kilmartin had served as Wing Commander Operations at HQ No. 84 Group having previously commanded the Hornchurch Wing.

Two weeks later the Typhoons of No. 136 Airfield were joined by Nos 183 and 609 Squadrons, bringing the total number of Typhoon squadrons to four. Some of the squadrons rotated through Llanbedr in Wales to take part in an armament practice camp. The result was that No. 193 Squadron did not return to Thorney Island and No. 198 Squadron then joined No. 609 Squadron to form No. 123 Airfield commanded by Wing Commander Desmond Scott, a twenty-five-year-old New Zealander who would soon become the youngest group captain in the RNZAF. Scott had just been awarded a DSO following his tour as wing leader at RAF Tangmere to add to his DFC and bar, which he had received for his success as a Hurricane pilot while serving with No. 3 Squadron.

Typhoons of No. 609 Squadron operated as part of No. 123 Wing at Thorney Island during the period of D-Day operations.

It would be these two airfields, soon to be renamed Nos 123 and 136 Wings, with four squadrons of Typhoons, which would operate together at Thorney Island during the final build-up to D-Day, taking part in offensive operations across the Channel, specifically against communications targets and V-1 flying bomb sites in northern France.

As Wing Commander Flying of No. 136 Wing was the legendary Wing Commander Billy Drake, one of the most experienced RAF fighter pilots at the time. Born in London, Drake had joined the RAF in 1936 and had flown Hurricanes with No. 1 Squadron during the Battle of France. His first three successes came in the skies over northern France before he was shot down in May 1940, after which he returned to the UK to recover from his injuries. Having returned to operations he carried out low-level fighter reconnaissance duties with the newly formed No. 421 Flight. Further claims followed, for which he was awarded the DFC, before Drake was given command of No. 128 Squadron in West Africa and then No. 112 Squadron in the Western Desert. More decorations followed, a DSO and a bar to his DFC, and he was then posted to Malta in 1943 where he commanded a wing. Having returned to the UK at the end of the year, Billy Drake was given command of the Typhoon wing at Thorney Island,

Commanding No. 123 Wing at Thorney Island on D-Day was Wing Commander Richard Brooker. A former school master, Brooker had previously flown Hurricanes during the Battle of Britain and had commanded a squadron in Singapore.

which he would lead during the build-up to the Allied invasion.

One of the largest *Ramrods* was flown on 26 April when Billy Drake led two squadrons of Typhoons from Thorney Island, Nos 164 and 183 Squadrons, plus two more squadrons of Typhoons from Needs Oar Point, led by Wing Commander Denys Gillam, on a low-level attack against a V-1 site. The raid was a great success, without any Typhoon losses, and this raid marked the first of a number of large-scale efforts by the Typhoon squadrons against specific targets of key importance.

When Drake was posted to the Fighter Leaders' School at Milfield as the Chief Instructor at the end of April 1944, the position of Wing Commander Flying of No. 136 Wing was given to the young Wing Commander Mike Bryan. Bryan had previously flown Whirlwinds and Hurricanes prior to the Typhoon when he was given command of No. 198 Squadron in August 1943. By the time he took command of the wing at Thorney Island, Bryan had been awarded a DFC and bar.

Commanding No. 123 Wing during the final build-up to D-Day was the vastly experienced Wing Commander Richard Brooker. A former school master, Brooker joined the RAF before the outbreak of the Second World War and had flown Hurricanes with No. 56 Squadron during the Battle of Britain, achieving his first success on 13 July 1940. He had then commanded No. 1 Squadron during the following year and was awarded the DFC before he was posted to the Far East where he commanded No. 232 Squadron in Singapore. During the subsequent retreat through the East Indies to Australia, Brooker had added more successes to his total and was awarded a bar to his DFC. He then commanded an Australian Kittyhawk squadron before returning to the UK when he was given command of No. 123 Wing at Thorney Island.

One pilot serving with No. 183 Squadron during this period at Thorney Island was Squadron Leader The Honourable Felix Scarlett. On 3 May Scarlett took a Typhoon to RAF Northolt to meet King George VI, who was carrying out a visit to Northolt to inspect a number of the RAF's latest aircraft types. Just over a week later, Scarlett survived a nasty incident when his Typhoon was hit by flak during an attack against an enemy radar site. His aircraft caught fire and he prepared to bale out. Having jettisoned his canopy the fire went out at that point and Scarlett decided to remain with the aircraft and fly it back to Thorney; no doubt it was a cold and draughty flight back to base!

Towards the end of May the Typhoon pilots turned their attention to the coastal radar sites. These were extremely hazardous missions for the pilots as evinced on one day, 24 May, when three Typhoons of No. 198 Squadron attacked a radar site at Cap de la Hague. The German troops on the ground watched as the Typhoons made their attack very low and from a valley. One aircraft was hit by 37mm flak, which practically shot off the tail. The pilot, however, managed to maintain some sort of control to press home his attack. He dived below the height of the radar structure and then fired his rockets at the very last moment and then tried to clear the structure. Another aircraft, in trying to avoid the damaged Typhoon, clipped the fuselage and both aircraft crashed into the installation. The radar site was destroyed but the two pilots, Flying Officer Harold Freeman and Flight Sergeant Edward Vallely, were killed. During another attack against a radar site, this time against a site near Torcy on 28 May, the commanding officer of No. 164 Squadron, Squadron Leader H Russell, was hit by flak. Russell managed to bale out of his aircraft and was taken as a prisoner of war but it was yet another loss to Thorney Island.

Despite the losses, a number of these radar sites had been successfully destroyed by D-Day. There were also air-to-air successes for the Typhoon pilots. One example was on 29 May when the Canadian Flying Officer 'Newfy' Taylor of No. 183 Squadron was scrambled from Thorney Island to intercept low-flying enemy Messerschmitt Bf109s on an intruder mission across the Channel. During the action, Taylor shot down two of the Bf109s to the south of the Isle of Wight. Sadly, 'Newfy' Taylor would be killed just days later; he was twenty-five years old.

The invasion was now just a matter of days away and the intensity of the operations was continuing to increase. An example is highlighted on 1 June, which for the Typhoon pilots of No. 609 Squadron, in particular, proved to be very busy. The squadron was on task at first light when eight Typhoons, led by the squadron commander, Squadron Leader Ingle, took off at 5.45 a.m. for a mission, known to the squadron pilots as one of 'Ingle's Tours', over the Dutch islands. Four of the Typhoons reached land between Walcheren and Schouwen islands where they encountered two coasters, one of 600 tons and the other 200 tons. The four Typhoons attacked the larger of the two and all scored hits against the ship and it was left smoking in the water. Continuing south-westerly, two of the Typhoons then attacked a stationary ship of around 500 tons, which turned out to be a flak ship, while the other two Typhoons attacked a tender vessel close by. The squadron commander's aircraft was hit by flak during his attack on the ship as all the enemy's fire seemed to concentrate on him. His Typhoon suffered extensive damage to his spinner and another cannon shell hit his port wheel bay, firing the primary fuel tank and exploding the spare starter cartridges, which in turn set fire to the aircraft wiring and was melting the port main fuel tank breather pipe and was now starting to burn continuously. Ingle pulled up to a height of 2,000 feet and turned out to sea, fully expecting his fuel tanks to blow up, and started heading back towards Hornchurch for an emergency landing, escorted by his wing men.

Meanwhile, the other four Typhoons, two equipped as fighter-bombers and two as fighter escorts, approached land at Blakenberge and found a 200-ton trawler between Knocke and Niuwe Sluis. One Typhoon attacked the trawler and observed hits all over the vessel followed by extensive smoke. The four Typhoons then continued and found six coasters, ranging in size between 600 tons and 1,000 tons, between Westkapelle and Flushing. At the same time flak started to open up on the four aircraft. One Typhoon pressed home a most determined attack against the lead vessel, scoring several hits, but was hit during the final stages of his run-in and the aircraft started losing hydraulic oil. The pilot turned for home, using the shore dykes for protection, and eventually made a successful belly-landing back home with the aircraft's hydraulic oil supply exhausted.

There were two more scrambles for the squadron during the morning, without incident, before two more Typhoons, led by Flight Lieutenant Johnnie Wells, took-off soon after mid-day and were tasked to orbit overhead base at 1,800 feet, in case there was any activity observed coming in from across the Channel. It was not long before the Typhoon pilots spotted three enemy aircraft and then more. Wells identified the aircraft as twelve Focke-Wulf FW190s and engaged the leaders and opened fire at range in an attempt to get the formation to break. It did not work and so Wells closed to 200 yards and opened fire on one of the FW190s, hitting it before attacking the next. Unfortunately for Wells, his wingman, Flying Officer Davies, had not heard his 'tally-ho' and had become distracted by bomb bursts below and attacked at least six FW190s carrying out an attack. He chased the formation out to sea, firing as he went and scored hits against the lead aircraft. He kept chasing the aircraft but two of the FW190s had now turned on him, and so he had to break off his attack to avoid being shot down before he eventually landed back at base; it had been a hectic hour.

During the afternoon the squadron mounted three more patrols over the airfield, all without incident, and then a patrol over Dover during the evening before last light. The day had seen eight different patrols and sorties for the squadron, and a number of claims made by the squadron's pilots during the two eventful missions earlier; it had been quite a day!

The following day there was a significant loss to Thorney Island during the afternoon when the commanding officer of No. 198 Squadron, Squadron Leader John Niblett, was shot down and killed while leading his squadron alongside Typhoons of No. 609 Squadron against a radar site near Dieppe. Niblett was the only loss from a force of eighteen Typhoons taking part in the raid but it was, once again, a notable loss to the airfield. His place as the commanding officer of the squadron was taken by Squadron Leader Idwal Davies who had been serving as a flight commander with No. 609 Squadron and he was now promoted instantly and posted across the airfield to assume command of his new squadron; sadly, however, Davies too would not survive the month and was killed during the early afternoon of 22 June when he was shot down by flak near Cherbourg.

On D-Day, 6 June, the Thorney wings were tasked to destroy German armoured units in the immediate vicinity of the invasion area and the roving Typhoons were responsible for one of the most devastating attacks of the day when the pilots spotted German armour moving along the roads towards Caen from the south-east of the town. It was the Panzer Lehr Division, which had been ordered to move by daylight, something not at all popular amongst the crews. The weather conditions were ideal for the Typhoons and there were no enemy fighters in the area, which meant that the Typhoon pilots could press home a devastating attack. This initial attack was followed up during the day with further attacks against the Panzer column. However, while the Typhoons enjoyed much success with the destruction of many armoured vehicles during the day, there were also losses. Around midday the Typhoons of No. 183 Squadron, led by Squadron Leader Scarlett, were carrying out a low-level attack against the column when they were attacked by an estimated dozen Messerschmitt Bf109s. During the following air action, three of the Typhoons were shot down; all the pilots were killed. One of the casualties was one of the flight commanders, twenty-two-year-old Flight Lieutenant Rhys Evans from Monmouthshire; he is buried in the Bayeux War Cemetery. One of the other pilots killed was 'Newfy' Taylor, who had enjoyed success just a few days before when he shot down two Bf109s in one sortie, and the other was another Canadian, twenty-two-year-old Flying Officer Melsom Gee. It was a tragic blow for the squadron.

Later in the afternoon, around 6.30 p.m., the Typhoons of No. 164 Squadron were on their third fighter sweep over the beachhead when they came under attack from Focke-Wulf FW190s to the north-east of Caen. One of the attackers was shot down by Squadron Leader Percy Beake but, sadly, one of the Typhoons was shot down, killing the Australian Flying Officer Alfred Roberts. Roberts was the third victim of the day for the Luftwaffe ace *Hauptmann* Herbert Huppertz, although Huppertz would himself be killed in action just two days later after claiming his seventieth victim of the war, which brought him the posthumous award of the Oak Leaves to his Knight's Cross.

The pattern for the Typhoons was much the same over the following few days whenever the weather allowed. Soon after midday on 8 June, Mike Bryan led eight Typhoons of No. 164 Squadron over the invasion area in support of the advancing Allied troops when the Typhoons were attacked by a dozen Messerschmitt Bf109s to the south of Caen; one of the Bf109s was shot down, shared between Flight Lieutenant Arthur Todd and Flight Sergeant Dick Wilson, and two more were reported as damaged, without the Typhoons suffering any losses. Later in the afternoon, the Typhoons of No. 198 Squadron were operating in the area of Caen when one aircraft, flown by Flight Sergeant James Milne, was hit by flak. Although Milne had lost his engine, he attempted to glide back across the Allied lines but he was unable to make it and was hit once again before his aircraft crashed to the north of Caen; James Milne was killed.

The weather then deteriorated on 9 June, which resulted in a significant reduction in Allied sorties flown and at times brought air operations to a halt. However, once the weather had improved, operations soon continued. Sadly, No. 136 Wing suffered a devastating loss during a low-level attack against German troop positions on 10 June when its wing leader, Wing Commander Mike Bryan, was shot down by flak and killed; he was just twenty-one years old and is buried in the Bretteville-sur-Laize Canadian war cemetery to the south of Caen.

During the early morning on 14 June the Typhoons of No. 198 Squadron were providing air support for the British Army's 50th Division's thrust in the Tilly-sur-Seulles to Lingevres area, on the western flank of the Allied advance into Normandy, when two aircraft fell to intense German flak with the loss of Pilot Officer Ron Crouch; the other pilot managed to force-land and survive.

As temporary runways were being rapidly prepared in Normandy, the Typhoons were able to land so that they could re-fuel and re-arm. The first squadron to leave Thorney to operate from across the Channel was No. 609 Squadron, which moved to Bazenville (B.2) on 18 June. It was at the same time that the three other squadrons left Thorney Island for Funtington; they would all cross the Channel in July.

The Typhoons were replaced by Mosquito VIs of No. 140 Wing, part of No. 2 Group, which moved in from their former base at Gravesend on the same day that the Typhoons had left Thorney Island. The Mosquito wing consisted of three squadrons – Nos 21, 464 and 487 Squadrons. Sadly, one notable loss to No. 21 Squadron occurred soon after the squadron arrived at Thorney Island when, on the night of 22 June, a Mosquito flown by Flight Lieutenant The Honourable Michael Wedgwood Benn, the brother of a man who would later become a Labour member of parliament and government minister, Anthony Wedgwood Benn, crashed on landing at Thorney Island after returning from a night operation across the Channel. Although he survived the crash, Michael Wedgwood Benn sadly later died from his injuries.

Soon after, during the night of 24/25 June, the squadron lost two more aircraft. One of the Mosquitos was flown by the legendary night-fighter ace, Wing Commander Bob Braham, during a patrol over the North Sea to Denmark. Flying with his navigator, the Australian Flight Lieutenant Don Walsh, their aircraft was shot down but Braham managed to crash-land the aircraft along the coast and the crew was taken as prisoners of war. At the time of his capture, Braham was still only twenty-four years old. His first success had occurred back in August 1940 while flying Blenheims with No. 29 Squadron during the Battle of Britain, after which he had gone on to be credited with at least twenty-nine enemy aircraft destroyed – achieved while flying Blenheims, Beaufighters and Mosquitos – for which he was awarded a DSO and two bars and a DFC and two bars; a remarkable achievement. After his capture Braham then remained a prisoner before returning to the UK at the end of the war.

The Mosquito wing would remain at Thorney Island until February 1945 during which time the wing mainly carried out night intruder missions across north-west Europe, disrupting enemy movements and destroying enemy lines of communications, as the Allies pushed deeper towards Germany. These night raids were interspersed with daylight raids against specific key targets such as the extremely successful daylight attack against the Gestapo headquarters and barracks located in the village of Bonneuil Matours in western France on 14 July, led by Group Captain Peter Wykeham-Barnes. There was a similar attack on 1 August against Gestapo barracks at Poiters, and Wykeham-Barnes again led the wing against the Gestapo headquarters at Aarhus on 31 October. This latter raid involved twenty-four Mosquitos, in four boxes of six aircraft, escorted by Mustangs, flying a round-trip of more than 1,000 miles. The raid was a success, taking the enemy defences by surprise, with the loss of just one aircraft.

While the wing enjoyed success in its daylight role, there were also losses and one example was on 22 August when Wing Commander Gordon Panitz, the twenty-eight-year-old Australian and commander of No. 464 Squadron, was lost over Le Creusot; he is buried in the Bona Communal Cemetery to the north-east of Nevers. Amongst their other tasks, the Thorney Mosquitos also supported the airborne assault on Arnhem in September as part of Operation *Market* and they also enjoyed some success against V-1 flying bombs. Bad weather during the winter, and fog, often meant there were days when operations were cancelled. Then, at the beginning of February 1945, the wing crossed the Channel to operate from Rosières-en-Santerre (B.87). Thorney Island then became home to squadrons of the Fleet Air Arm. Some of these FAA squadrons, which were serving under No. 16 Group, Coastal Command, had remained at Thorney Island during 1944 while the 2nd TAF had operated from the airfield.

By the end of the war there were only naval units at Thorney Island but in 1946 RAF strike and anti-submarine units of Coastal Command returned. At the end of 1947 the airfield was transferred to Fighter Command and Thorney Island was then home to RAF Meteor jet fighters until 1950 when the airfield was transferred again, this time to Flying Training Command. Throughout the 1950s the airfield was home to No. 2 Air Navigation School and, for the latter half of the decade, a detachment of air-sea rescue helicopters. In 1962 Thorney Island was transferred yet again and this time the airfield became home to Hastings, Beverleys and Argosies of Transport Command and a detachment of Whirlwind search and rescue helicopters. In 1967 the Hercules aircraft arrived and then, in 1970, the Andover. However, their stay was short-lived as defence cuts resulted in the announcement that Thorney Island was to close.

A Typhoon of No. 609 Squadron with its ground personnel. The squadron arrived at Thorney Island at the beginning of April 1944 and operated from the airfield throughout the D-Day operations.

After Transport Command left Thorney Island in 1975 the airfield closed in March 1976. Part of the site was transferred to the Royal Navy but plans for use by the navy, and then later as a general aviation airfield for Portsmouth, both fell through. For a short period some of the hangars were used by Britten-Norman to store their Islander aircraft but there was no further use of the airfield. Thorney Island was then transferred to the army during the early 1980s and since 1984 has been a base for the Royal Artillery. It is now Baker Barracks and the site is home to 12 and 47 Regiments of the Royal Artillery with 12 Regiment providing close air defence protection and 47 Regiment being one of only two regiments in the Royal Artillery that, through the use of unmanned air systems, provide the British Army's 'eye in the sky' in support of land forces on operations.

Although Thorney Island is easily found from the A27, or from the A259 that runs east-west through the village of Emsworth, it is not accessible to the public as a military check point before reaching the former airfield prevents any access to the public unless by prior arrangement.

Squadron	Dates at Thorney Island	Aircraft type
164 Squadron	15 Mar–17 Jun 44	Typhoon I
193 Squadron	15 Mar–6 Apr 44	Typhoon I
198 Squadron	6 Apr–18 Jun 44	Typhoon I
183 Squadron	1 Apr–18 Jun 44	Typhoon I
609 Squadron	1 Apr–18 Jun 44	Typhoon I
21 Squadron	18 Jun 44–6 Feb 45	Mosquito VI
464 Squadron RAAF	18 Jun 44–5 Feb 45	Mosquito VI
487 Squadron RNZAF	18 Jun 44–2 Feb 45	Mosquito VI

Westhampnett

Now the site of Goodwood Airfield, Westhampnett was once an active airfield of the 2nd TAF and home to Typhoons during the period of D-Day operations. Situated just 2 miles to the north-east of Chichester, Westhampnett was another airfield developed just before the Second World War when the Air Ministry needed to increase its number of airfields. Within the Goodwood Estate, home to the Duke of Richmond for over 300 years, a large area of land was identified as suitable for development as an emergency landing ground for aircraft based at nearby Tangmere.

The site was used as an emergency landing ground but in the summer of 1940 it was upgraded to satellite status and was then increasingly used by Hurricanes from Tangmere. Westhampnett had four grass runways with the longest being 1,500 yards running in a south-east to north-west direction. The second longest ran from the south-west to the north-east and was 1,100 yards. The two smaller runways, 1,000 yards and 900 yards, ran from north-south and east-west respectively. A basic watch tower was situated in the north-east corner of the airfield. Personnel were initially accommodated in bell tents with aircraft dispersed around the site and serviced in Blister hangars but the limited facilities meant that only one squadron could operate from the airfield at any one time.

During the Battle of Britain Westhampnett was one of the most southerly located airfields, which meant that reaction time for the pilots and ground personnel was often very short. However, because it was one of the most westerly of No. 11 Group's airfields, there was a gradual reduction in the intensity

Typhoons and pilots of No. 245 Squadron pictured at Westhampnett during the early months of 1944 when the squadron formed part of No. 124 Airfield. Westhampnett suffered from poor drainage and so better dispersals had to be constructed as did a new hangar so that routine maintenance could be carried out.

of operations from Westhampnett when the Luftwaffe turned its attention to London. After the battle Westhampnett was home to various squadrons operating in a variety of roles and over the next year or so the airfield underwent further development, including the construction of a tarmac perimeter track, an extension to the shortest runway to 1,000 yards and improvements to the airfield's accommodation by the addition of Nissen huts. During 1942 Westhampnett became a USAAF station but by the early months of 1943 the residents were two RAF Spitfire V squadrons.

By the summer of 1943 there were two Spitfire XII squadrons at Westhampnett – Nos 41 and 91 Squadrons – which were initially used to combat the Luftwaffe's low-level fighter-bomber attacks on coastal targets in southern England but as these started to decrease the Spitfires were increasingly used to fly coastal reconnaissance sorties, fighter sweeps over northern France and to carry out support for bombers of No. 2 Group attacking targets across the Channel and also for providing fighter escort for Typhoon fighter-bombers of No. 83 Group.

The Spitfires left Westhampnett at the beginning of October and were replaced by Typhoons of No. 121 Airfield, part of No. 83 Group – consisting of Nos 174, 175 and 245 Squadrons – which arrived from Lydd. Commanding No. 121 Airfield was Wing Commander C S Morice and leading the Typhoons as Wing Commander Flying was the twenty-six-year-old Canadian Wing

Commander Bob Davidson who had just been given command of the wing after previously commanding No. 175 Squadron. A veteran of the campaigns in the Western Desert and the Far East, Davidson now had a DFC in recognition of his achievement and he would soon add to his personal score while operating from Westhampnett, which brought his total to four confirmed kills.

This Typhoon wing, with the exception of some very short periods detached away, would remain at Westhampnett until the beginning of April 1944. The squadrons took part in numerous ground-attack sorties and in January 1944 the Westhampnett Typhoons were gradually converted to carry rockets. The pilots of No. 174 Squadron went to Eastchurch to carry out their training in firing rocket projectiles. The following month it was the turn of No. 175 Squadron to go to Eastchurch; No. 245 Squadron would convert later. The Typhoons were now able to carry out dive-bombing attacks against key ground installations, such as V-1 flying-bomb sites, radar stations and communications targets in preparation for the Allied invasion of Europe.

One notable raid, which was supported by the Typhoons of Westhampnett, was Operation *Jericho* on 18 February 1944. Sixteen Typhoons of Nos 174 and 245 Squadrons, eight from each squadron, escorted eighteen Mosquitos of No. 2 Group that had taken off from Hunsdon and were being led by Group Captain 'Pick' Pickard to attack the Gestapo headquarters at Amiens where some 700 members of the French Resistance were reported as being held. The plan was for the Mosquitos to attack in three waves, with the first two waves given specific targets and the third wave being used as a mobile reserve with the task of attacking anything missed by the first two waves. Poor weather prevented a third Typhoon squadron at Manston from getting airborne on time but the two Westhampnett squadrons had managed to get airborne, despite the weather, and joined up with the Mosquitos over the Channel. The poor weather en route had meant that only fifteen of the Mosquitos were able to reach the target but the attack was carried out with pin-point accuracy and the walls of the prison were successfully breached allowing more than 250 of the prisoners to escape. Unfortunately, though, a hundred prisoners were killed during the raid and the leader of Operation *Jericho*, 'Pick' Pickard, and his navigator, Flight Lieutenant John Broadley, were killed when their Mosquito

Ground crew take a well-earned rest at a NAAFI wagon pictured in front of a Typhoon of No. 245 Squadron during early 1944.

was shot down by two Focke-Wulf FW190s. One other Mosquito was also shot down and two Typhoons of No. 174 Squadron were also lost with one pilot killed, Flight Sergeant Henry Brown, and the other pilot taken as a prisoner of war.

Another notable raid for the Typhoons was during the afternoon of 16 March when Wing Commander Charles Green, Wing Commander Flying at No. 121 Airfield, led sixteen aircraft, taken from all three squadrons at Westhampnett, on a low-level Rodeo to the Paris area. The Typhoons, fitted with long-range fuel tanks, crossed the French coast near St Valery at 8,000 feet and then descended to low-level. The Typhoons then carried out a number of attacks against enemy airfields and military establishments, causing havoc and achieving much success, and claiming at least five enemy aircraft destroyed; one Typhoon was lost with the pilot, Flying Officer Charles Austin, killed when his aircraft was shot down by flak to the south of Etampes.

With three squadrons now operating continuously over the Channel, Westhampnett had to undergo some modifications and improvements during early 1944. Like other airfields in the area, Westhampnett suffered from poor drainage and so better dispersals had to be built as did a new hangar to carry out essential and routine aircraft maintenance. On 1 April No. 121 Airfield moved to Holmsley South and exchanged places with the Canadians of No. 144 Airfield. The three new squadrons – Nos 441, 442 and 443 Squadrons – had only recently formed and were now replacing their Spitfire Vs, which they had received only a matter of weeks before, with MkIXs and none of the squadrons were yet declared operational.

Although the squadrons remained at Westhampnett for less than three weeks, there was enough time to complete their training and No. 443 Squadron achieved its first success from Westhampnett on 19 April. The commanding officer, Squadron Leader Wally McLeod, a veteran of the Malta campaign and with at least thirteen kills to his name, for which he had been awarded a DFC and bar, scored the squadron's first success. Having completed their training, the Canadians then moved out. They were replaced by just one squadron, No. 184 Squadron, equipped with the Typhoon and designated No. 129 Airfield, led by Wing Commander D S C Macdonald, as part of No. 83 Group – even though it was a single squadron – which arrived from Odiham on 23 April.

The fact that the airfield was grass continued to make it difficult to operate from when wet, particularly with some of the more heavily armed aircraft, which meant that Westhampnett was never suitable for aircraft such as the Mosquito. It also meant that it was difficult to operate more than one squadron at a time in support of the Allied landings and so No. 184 Squadron operated from Westhampnett alone during the final build-up to D-Day.

On D-Day, 6 June, the squadron carried out rocket attacks against strong points and defensive positions on or around the beachhead. They were high-risk sorties and despite its successes the squadron also suffered losses. During the late afternoon of the following day, 7 June, eight Typhoons of No. 184 Squadron, led by Flight Lieutenant 'Dutch' Holland, were carrying out a rocket attack against railway marshalling yards at Mezidon when the pilots ran into severe anti-aircraft fire, which brought down three of the Typhoons. One of the pilots, twenty-three-year-old Flight Sergeant John Rowland, was killed, although the other two pilots survived, including 'Dutch' Holland who spent the next two months evading capture before later returning to flying operations with the 2nd TAF.

The weather then deteriorated on 9 June, which resulted in a significant reduction in Allied sorties flown and at times brought air operations to a halt. Soon after, on 17 June, No. 184 Squadron left Westhampnett for Holmsley South and a week later crossed the Channel to operate from Plumetot (B.10). Westhampnett was then briefly home to three squadrons of Spitfire Vs – Nos 130, 303 and 402 Squadrons – although initially the squadrons could not take part in operations. A strong gale had blown up in the Channel unexpectedly during the early hours of 19 June and this brought daylight operations to a standstill for the next three days. However, by 22 June the weather had cleared for operations to resume and for the next week the squadrons flew patrols over the beachhead and took part in bomber escort duties. At the end of the month the squadrons moved out and Spitfire XIIs of No. 41 Squadron moved in for a few days to help counter the V-1 raids against southern England before departing for Friston.

During August and September Westhampnett was home to three Spitfire IX squadrons – Nos 118, 124 and 303 Squadrons (which had returned from Merston) – which all carried out bomber escort as the Allies pushed further and further towards Germany. These squadrons left Westhampnett on 25 September and, just like other airfields in the south of England, the sky around Westhampnett was suddenly quiet.

In November No. 83 Group Support Unit arrived with the task of providing replacement aircraft and pilots for the 2nd TAF's front-line Spitfire and Mustang units. Once again the weather and poor drainage meant that Westhampnett was not well placed to provide support during the winter months and the Support Unit moved out early in 1945. Westhampnett was then placed on care and maintenance and the airfield was transferred to the Supreme Headquarters Allied Expeditionary Forces (SHAEF) as a rear headquarters.

After the war the airfield briefly opened for flying but was soon placed on care and maintenance once again. As a motor racing enthusiast, the Duke of Richmond and Gordon noted that the former airfield offered potential as a motor racing circuit, in particular the tarmac perimeter track, and the site was renamed and became home to the Goodwood Motor Racing circuit in 1948 to host Britain's very first post-war motor race as the spiritual successor to Brooklands. For the next seventeen years Goodwood was used as a racing circuit until the cost of providing the ever-improving safety features that were now required for motor racing became too high. The site was then reverted back for use as an airfield and developed by the Goodwood Terrena

The former wartime airfield of Westhampnett is now an active flying club within the Goodwood complex. A privately owned Percival Pembroke sits proudly at this former RAF airfield and this picture was taken from the Goodwood Flying Club at the south-east corner of the airfield and looking north-westwards with the white markers lining the main runway on the left of the picture.

Company, which made best use of the former RAF facilities, combined with the construction of a new hangar and new accommodation, for use as a flying club.

The former airfield is now part of the Goodwood complex, which includes the motor racing circuit and horse racing, and remains active as a flying club. The racing circuit completely encircles the airfield, which now has three grass runways and there are thousands of aircraft movements each year. Some of the former RAF buildings remain such as the large sheds and the old air traffic control tower. The Goodwood Aero Club offers its members the opportunity to relive wartime missions with unique access to Warbirds and pilots at the Goodwood Revival and offers pleasure flights in vintage aircraft. Goodwood also hosts an annual Aviation Exhibition, which enables manufacturers and agents of fixed wing and rotary aircraft to showcase their latest innovative aircraft design, as an addition to its annual Festival of Speed.

Goodwood has a huge passion for aviation and the site is well worth a visit. If travelling from the north take the A286 to the village of East Lavant and then travel eastwards on the Fordwater Road, which then becomes New Road and you will soon see the airfield on your right. Then turn right into

The former air traffic control tower at Westhampnett can be found alongside the Goodwood racing circuit at the eastern edge of the complex.

Claypit Lane and the entrance to the airfield is on your right. If travelling from the west stay on the A27 Chichester bypass until the eastern side of the town and then follow signs northwards to the village of Westhampnett and then take Claypit Lane to the entrance to the aerodrome. If travelling from the east, before you reach Chichester, take the A285 Stame Road northwards. After less than a mile take New Road to the left and follow this west for about 2 miles until you come to a roundabout and turn left into Claypit Lane. The entrance to the aerodrome is then on your right. The address is: Goodwood Airfield, Goodwood, Chichester, West Sussex PO18 0PH. The telephone number is 01243 755000.

Entrance to the aerodrome is through the underpass, which is only big enough for cars. Turn left and drive down to the Aero Club at the Goodwood Flying School where you can park and get a wonderful view across the airfield, particularly from the café, which is open to the public. Outside the Aero Club you will see the bronze statue of Douglas Bader looking across the airfield, which was unveiled in 2001 to honour the legendary fighter pilot who served at Westhampnett during the Second World War. From here you can walk to the old air traffic control tower, which is situated just on the other side of the racing track and can be reached by using the pedestrian underpass.

The bronze statue of Douglas Bader looking out across the former airfield of Westhampnett can be found adjacent to the Goodwood Aero Club.

Squadron	Dates at Westhampnett	Aircraft type
41 Squadron	21 Jun–4 Oct 43	Spitfire XII
91 Squadron	28 Jun–4 Oct 43	Spitfire XII
174 Squadron	10 Oct 43–1 Apr 44	Typhoon I
175 Squadron	9 Oct 43–1 Apr 44	Typhoon I
245 Squadron	10 Oct 43–1 Apr 44	Typhoon I
441 Squadron RCAF	1–12 Apr 44	Spitfire IX
442 Squadron RCAF	1–22 Apr 44	Spitfire IX
443 Squadron RCAF	8–22 Apr 44	Spitfire IX
184 Squadron	23 Apr–17 Jun 44	Typhoon I
130 Squadron	19–27 Jun 44	Spitfire V
303 'Warsaw' Squadron	18–26 Jun 44	Spitfire V
402 Squadron RCAF	19–27 Jun 44	Spitfire V
41 Squadron	28 Jun–4 Jul 44	Spitfire XII
124 Squadron	9 Aug–25 Sep 44	Spitfire IX
303 'Warsaw' Squadron	9 Aug–25 Sep 44	Spitfire IX
118 Squadron	29 Aug–25 Sep 44	Spitfire IX

CHAPTER FOUR

Airfields of Hampshire

The beautiful county of Hampshire on the southern coast of England, with its blend of national parks and seaside resorts, has a strong maritime history but it has also witnessed some historic events since the birth of aviation in this country. Farnborough, in the north of the county, had been the location for Samuel Cody's first sustained aeroplane flight in the British Isles, which took place in 1908, and was then the birthplace of the Royal Flying Corps in 1912. Being situated in the south of England meant that Hampshire then saw a number of airfields developed in the period after the First World War as aviation became popular, fashionable and commercial as well, of course, as a military capability, and there has always been a strong naval aviation presence in the county since the First World War. Then, during the 1930s, in response to the threat posed by the newly formed Luftwaffe in Germany, the Air Ministry Works Directorate was given the task of developing new airfields. Although many of the new airfields were popping up all over eastern and south-eastern England, Hampshire was also an important part of the plan and airfields such as Odiham and Middle Wallop were developed. The county is also proud to have been the location for the first flight of the Spitfire, which took place at Eastleigh (now the site of Southampton Airport) in 1936, and during the Second World War, after the Supermarine Works was destroyed in September 1940, design and manufacture of Spitfire parts was dispersed around the county.

During the early period of the Second World War the airfields located in Hampshire had been allocated to a training or support role, or had been allocated to the Fleet Air Arm, but their proximity to the major ports of Southampton and Portsmouth, combined with incorrect German intelligence, meant that some of these airfields had come under attack by the Luftwaffe, in the belief that the airfields were being used as fighter bases by Fighter Command. After the Battle of Britain, Hampshire's twenty-seven military airfields, including five advanced landing grounds, were used for a variety of purposes and by early 1944 activity had reached a peak. Eight of these airfields and one advanced landing ground were used by the 2nd TAF during preparations for the Allied invasion of Europe.

Like all other counties, many airfields have long disappeared but Hampshire still boasts a number of significant airfields used for a variety of purposes. These include military airfields such as Odiham, the only airfield in the county currently used by the RAF and it has been home of the Chinook helicopter for some years, and Middle Wallop, which is home to the Army Air Corps. Some of the airfields later became airports, such as Blackbushe (formally Hartford Bridge), Farnborough and Eastleigh, and other sites have since become better known for other recreational purposes such as Thruxton, which, although still used as an airfield, is probably better known for its motor racing.

Many of Hampshire's airfields were not used by the 2nd TAF during the Second World War and so are not included in this chapter, although many were used by either the Americans or naval units instead; these include the airfields of Andover, Chilbolton, Gosport, Middle Wallop and Stoney Cross, and the advanced landing grounds of Lymington and Winkton. Also not included in this chapter are other ALGs that were either too far from the coast to be used during D-Day, such as Frost Hill Farm, or not deemed suitable for other reasons, such as Larks Barrow.

The New Forest, in particular, saw the height of wartime activity, not just its airfields, of which there were no fewer than twelve airfields and landing grounds in and around the immediate vicinity of the New Forest, but it was also a prime location for military action and the dense forest provided natural cover from the enemy's aerial reconnaissance. The area saw its busiest period during the build-up to D-Day when the New Forest was used to accommodate temporary camps for the army, when the number of troops vastly exceeded the number of local inhabitants, and local narrow roads had to be widened to allow use by tanks and other heavy vehicles; there is also evidence of concrete along the shores where the Mulberry Harbours were constructed. As for the former airfields, the thin top soils of the New Forest mean that some of the runways and building foundations have not yet been fully reclaimed by nature and although most of the tarmac and concrete areas have long been removed by the Forestry Commission, outlines and evidence of activity do sometimes remain.

Beaulieu

Now reverted to beautiful heathland in the heart of the New Forest, the airfield of Beaulieu was used by the 2nd TAF units during early 1944 and then by the Americans during the D-Day operations, and for a while became one of the busiest airfields in the south of England.

Situated just 5 miles to the north-east of Lymington, the origins of this airfield date back to before the First World War when the original site was developed at East Boldre and used by the New Forest Flying School. Beaulieu was then used by the Royal Flying Corps and then the Royal Air Force during the First World War and later as a civilian airfield during the 1930s but a new site, built on Hatchet Moor to the west of the original site, was then developed for use as a Second World War airfield as a satellite for Thorney Island.

The site was initially intended to be one of Hampshire's advanced landing grounds and the new airfield of Beaulieu was opened in August 1942 but it soon became apparent that a larger airfield was needed for the operation of heavy bombers and so Beaulieu was upgraded in status to a Class A bomber airfield. Three intersecting hardened runways were constructed, at 60 degrees to each other in a triangular pattern, and surrounded by a perimeter track, 50 feet wide, with some 50 hardened dispersal sites for the aircraft. The main runway of nearly 2,000 yards ran in an east-west direction and the two shorter runways of just under 1,400 yards in length ran from south-east to north-west and from the south-west to the north-east, which all gave the appearance of the letter 'A' when viewed from the air. There were two T-2 type hangars, one on the north-west part of the airfield, where the main technical site was located, and the other on the southern part of the airfield where a large number of the aircraft dispersals were located. The airfield's buildings were mainly Nissen huts of various sizes, which included many facilities for the 2,000 station personnel, all linked by a network of small roads, although a number of domestic accommodation sites were located away from the airfield.

As soon as the airfield was ready for use, a Liberator squadron of Coastal Command, No. 224 Squadron, moved in to help counter the U-Boat threat in the Bay of Biscay; this was in September 1942 and the squadron remained until the end of April 1943 when it moved to Cornwall. Beaulieu was then home to Liberators of Nos 53 and 311 Squadrons until the end of the year when the airfield was needed by the 2nd TAF.

The first 2nd TAF aircraft to arrive were Typhoons of No. 257 Squadron from Warmwell, which arrived in January 1944, followed by No. 263 Squadron from Fairwood Common. The first Typhoon operations from Beaulieu took place on 22 January, when eight aircraft of No. 257 Squadron carried out an attack against a 'Noball' V-1 site on the Cherbourg Peninsula, and the airfield was also used during the month by the nearby Ibsley Wing taking part in *Rodeos* across the Channel. No. 257 Squadron swapped places with No. 486 Squadron at the end of the month, with No. 257 Squadron moving to Tangmere and No. 486 Squadron moving in the other direction. The Beaulieu Typhoons then flew more sorties against the V-1 sites and at the end of February No. 486 Squadron moved to Drem in Scotland, followed a week later by No. 263 Squadron, which moved to Warmwell.

The airfield was then transferred to No. 10 Group ADGB and Beaulieu was prepared for the imminent arrival of American units. By the time the Americans arrived, the RAF units had moved out. As USAAF Station AAF 408, Beaulieu was then home to three P-47 Thunderbolt squadrons of the 365th Fighter Group of the US Ninth Air Force during the period leading up to, and then during, the D-Day operations when, on 6 June, the Thunderbolts were in action over Omaha beach. Their duties were to attack gun emplacements and communications facilities behind the bridgehead. Two of the Thunderbolts were lost during the day and the following day five more. It was a hard time for the Americans but the 365th Fighter Group was one of the most successful Thunderbolt groups in the US Ninth Air Force and its pilots claimed twenty-nine enemy aircraft destroyed during its time at Beaulieu, although twenty-four Thunderbolts had failed

This information board marks the eastern end of the main runway of the former airfield of Beaulieu and can be found on Beaulieu Heath just off the B3054.

to return. By the end of the month the Thunderbolts had crossed the Channel to operate from France and were replaced by B-26 Marauders, although these did not stay long and Beaulieu was handed back to the RAF at the end of September.

The airfield then remained empty until the Airborne Forces Experimental Establishment arrived in December 1944 and Beaulieu was then home to a mix of aircraft types, including RAF heavy bombers, such as the Lancaster and Halifax, and transport aircraft such as the Dakota, which were used to carry out a variety of experimental work. After the war the AFEE remained at Beaulieu until 1950 when its function had been absorbed by Boscombe Down. Beaulieu was then placed on care and maintenance and, although briefly nominated to be a standby base for the US 3rd Air Force during the 1950s, the airfield was finally closed at the end of 1959. The land was then taken over by the Forestry Commission and there is very little of the former airfield to be seen today, as most of the concreted areas have been removed and the vast area is now covered by heath land; although from the air the distinctive A-shaped layout of the runways can still be clearly seen.

This tarmac area on Beaulieu Heath is the only surviving part of the former runways and is now used by radio-controlled model aircraft enthusiasts.

The site of the former airfield can be found by travelling either from the Lymington direction, after about 5 miles when travelling north-eastwards along the B3054 Lyndhurst Road, or from Beaulieu. If travelling from Beaulieu, proceed westwards along the B3054 Hatchet Lane for about a mile. The road then forks at a small but tranquil gravel pit, popular in fine weather for visitors to the Forest, with the B3054 Lyndhurst Road continuing to the left and the B3055 Beaulieu Road to the right. The B3055 Beaulieu Road will take you along the northern edge of the former airfield and after about a mile, and just before the road takes a right hand bend, there is a footpath leading down to the remains of the perimeter track and this is the northern most point of the former airfield.

But the best option is to take the B3054 south-westwards from where the road forks at the gravel pit towards Lymington. The village of East Boldre, the site of the original airfield, is immediately off to your left but if you continue along the B3054 for about another mile you will see a gravel track turning off to the right at Beaulieu Heath. Take this track and follow it round to where you will find a small section of the eastern end of the main runway, which ran east-west. This tarmac area is the only surviving part of the former runways and the area is now used on a regular basis by model radio-controlled aircraft enthusiasts. There is also a board marking the former site, which also gives a brief history of RAF Beaulieu. Although the gravel track around the site marks the former perimeter track of the airfield, which traces a rather irregular shape of a hexagon with the vertices, or points, marking the end of the former runways, no buildings remain but the old water tower is still used by a local campsite.

Squadron	Dates at Beaulieu	Aircraft type
257 Squadron	20–31 Jan 44	Typhoon I
263 Squadron	23 Jan–6 Mar 44	Typhoon I
486 Squadron RNZAF	31 Jan–28 Feb 44	Typhoon I

Hartford Bridge

Now known as Blackbushe Airport but called Hartford Bridge during 1944, this airfield was home to Bostons and Mitchells of No. 2 Group and its Bostons were amongst the very first Allied aircraft over the invasion area on D-Day. Situated alongside the A30 between Camberley and Hook in the parish of Yateley, the land known as Hartford Bridge Flats was identified in 1941 as suitable for development as an airfield and heavy construction work began at the end of the year. Three concrete runways were constructed and Hartford Bridge opened on 1 November 1942 as an airfield of No. 70 Group.

Hartford Bridge was initially used by the Royal Aircraft Establishment, located at nearby Farnborough, for trials and development work while the final construction of the airfield took place. In March 1943 the airfield became home to No. 140 Squadron, a photo-reconnaissance unit equipped with photo-reconnaissance Spitfires, Blenheims and Venturas, and three months later No. 16 Squadron, equipped with tactical reconnaissance Mustangs, moved into Hartford Bridge; the two squadrons then became No. 34 (PR) Wing in preparation for the forthcoming Allied invasion of Europe.

The Blenheims were used for night reconnaissance but some missions were flown by the Venturas, together with Venturas from No. 21 Squadron, which had moved briefly to Hartford

Bostons from Hartford Bridge were among the very first Allied aircraft over the invasion area during the early hours of D-Day when they successfully laid a smoke screen ahead of the invasion force.

Bridge from Oulton, and in August No. 140 Squadron started to take delivery of Mosquitos and, the following month Spitfires, which then carried out photo-reconnaissance sorties over Europe. The low-level Mustangs of No. 16 Squadron were given the task of intercepting German fighter-bombers attacking the coastal towns along the south coast of England. In September the squadron started to take delivery of Spitfires and these were used to carry out photo-reconnaissance sorties at both high-level and low-level in preparation for D-Day.

By now Hartford Bridge was under the control of No. 2 Group and was used by a No. 2 Group wing, consisting of Bostons – Nos 88, 107 and 342 Squadrons – which were used relentlessly to bomb a wide range of targets including enemy airfields, railway marshalling yards and ammunition dumps as well as carrying out attacks against coastal targets, ports and enemy shipping. In October the squadrons took part in separate bombing raids against a number of electrical power stations and transformers in France; No. 88 Squadron attacked the station at Distre, No. 107 Squadron attacked Orléans and No. 342 Squadron attacked the station at Chevilly. Although the wing suffered losses due to ground defences, a number of transformers were destroyed or damaged, which caused severe disruption to the local communications networks.

All the Hartford Bridge squadrons were now part of the 2nd TAF and, in preparation for the Allied invasion of Europe, the photographic wing were busy ensuring that the essential photographs of northern France were as up to date as possible, which helped prepare the landing charts and maps for the planned invasion. Meanwhile, the Bostons were used for a number of bombing tasks but their main task during the latter weeks of the year was to carry out attacks against the emerging V-1 rocket sites, which had been identified in northern France. Under its new structure, the Bostons operated as No. 137 Airfield.

In February 1944 No. 107 Squadron left Hartford Bridge for nearby Lasham and was replaced by No. 226 Squadron, equipped with Mitchells, which arrived from Swanton Morley to carry out daylight raids on enemy communications targets and airfields. The Mitchells and Bostons tended to operate independently from each other, with the Mitchells of No. 226 Squadron often operating with Mitchells from Dunsfold, and the photo-reconnaissance Spitfires were now operating further afield over north-west Europe. No. 140 Squadron had now taken delivery of the improved Spitfire XI and technology had also improved to allow the squadron to also operate at night or in bad weather.

In April the PR wing moved to Northolt, leaving the units of No. 137 Airfield at Hartford Bridge. They were soon joined by the Spitfire XIVs of No. 322 (Dutch) Squadron, with the responsibility of carrying high-level defensive patrols against an increasing number of German reconnaissance aircraft that were operating at high altitude to gather as much intelligence as possible as the Allies made their final plans for the invasion of Europe. It was also during April that General Eisenhower, the Supreme Allied Commander, visited Hartford Bridge to congratulate the crews on their great effort so far and to update them on the planning for the forthcoming invasion.

In May the Spitfires were joined by Mosquito XIII night-fighters of No. 264 Squadron to form No. 141 Airfield. The Mosquitos were soon busy and a little over a week after their arrival at Hartford Bridge, on the night of 14/15 May, they were in action over the south-west of England when the Luftwaffe turned its attention to Bristol. One of the enemy bombers, a Junkers Ju88, was shot down near Alton by Flight Lieutenant Charles Ramsay and his radar operator, Flying Officer John Edgar, of No. 264 Squadron. Ramsay had joined the squadron just a matter of weeks before, having been awarded the DFC the previous year while flying Beaufighters with No. 153 Squadron in North Africa. The Ju88 crashed near Selborne, to the south-east of Alton, in Hampshire. It was Ramsay's third success of the war but unfortunately during the attack his Mosquito had been hit, killing his radar operator; John Edgar is buried in the Leadgate (St Ives) Churchyard in Durham.

The two designated airfields at Hartford Bridge subsequently became Nos 137 and 141 Wings respectively with the units of No. 137 Wing operating under No. 2 Group and No. 141 Wing operating as part of No. 85 Group. During the final weeks before D-Day the Bostons were used extensively to carry out numerous raids across the Channel, specifically to attack enemy defences while maintaining their operational tempo against the V-1 flying-bomb sites, and the Spitfires of No. 322 Squadron became increasingly used in offensive operations across northern France.

There was also an additional Mitchell flight at Hartford Bridge, which operated as part of No. 226 Squadron and was used to carry out specialist operations over northern France. The flight, known as the 'Ginger Mitchell Flight', made use of a French radio operator on board the aircraft, which was flown across the Channel where the radio operator could pick up transmissions being made by a network of special agents in France that were reporting on German troop movements. Normal Morse code transmission practices were considered too risky and so short voice transmissions were used instead, which used a narrow radio beam transmission that was difficult to detect on the ground but was more easily detected at height. The first of these specialist operations was flown from Hartford Bridge on 1 June, under the cover tasking of leaflet dropping, or 'Nickelling' as it was more commonly known, although the Mitchells did carry leaflets on board, and drop them, should an aircraft be subsequently shot down or had to make a forced-landing. From then on the normal concept of operations was for two Mitchells to get airborne each night in this specialist role, with each aircraft receiving transmissions from one agent on the ground.

On D-Day the two Boston squadrons from Hartford Bridge were amongst the very first Allied aircraft over the invasion area. They had been modified to carry smoke screen devices in their bomb bays and, despite a strong wind over the area, it was soon after 5.00 a.m. when the Bostons successfully laid a smoke screen ahead of the invasion force; No. 88 Squadron covered the

Now known as Blackbushe Airport, the former airfield of Hartford Bridge can be found alongside the A30 in northern Hampshire between Camberley and Hook.

eastern flank and No. 342 Squadron the western flank with a Boston arriving on task every ten minutes to keep a continuous screen over the invasion area. This all helped prevent the location of the force and to keep the German defences guessing as to when and where the actual landing would take place but it was a hazardous operation with each squadron losing an aircraft in the sea before the first troops had even gone ashore. The first aircraft lost was from No. 342 Squadron and flew into the sea around 6.30 a.m.; the crew of three was all killed. The second Boston, from No. 88 Squadron, was lost an hour later in similar circumstances; again, the crew were killed.

The weather then deteriorated on 9 June, which resulted in a significant reduction in Allied sorties flown and at times brought air operations to a halt. Better weather saw operations resume and the following day saw the 2nd TAF, including the Mitchells of No. 226 Squadron, carry out a successful attack against the headquarters of the commander of Panzer Group West, General Geyr von Schweppenburg, which was located in the Chateau de la Caine to the south-west of Caen. Poor weather had meant that the raid, which had originally been planned for the early afternoon, was delayed until the evening. Eighteen Mitchells of No. 226 Squadron led by the squadron's commanding officer Wing Commander Mitchell joined forces with fifty-three Mitchells of No. 139 Wing at Dunsfold and forty rocket-firing

Typhoons from Hurn and Holmsley South to carry out the raid. Each Mitchell carried a full 4,000lb bomb load and the attack was carried out from 12,000 feet, with the Typhoons operating at low-level, which resulted in the destruction of communications and signals equipment as well as many vehicles located in the grounds of the chateau. The raid was so successful that it would be more than two weeks before the headquarters would be fully functional again.

During the following days the Mitchells and Bostons from Hartford Bridge took part in further raids and were increasingly used for a variety of tasks, such as attacking strong points or hampering the German troop and tank movements, as the Allies started to break out of the beachhead and advance into Normandy. The night-fighter Mosquitos of No. 264 Squadron were also busy and during the night of 11/12 June claimed a Junkers Ju88 and a Focke-Wulf FW190 as destroyed; the squadron's 100th success of the war.

The following night the squadron was in action again when the night-fighter Mosquitos of No. 85 Group, including three crews of No. 141 Wing, enjoyed considerable success when nine Luftwaffe bombers were shot down. Two aircraft, both Junkers Ju188s, were shot down by No. 264 Squadron and another Ju188 was shot down by No. 410 Squadron. Then, on the night of 14/15 June, No. 264 Squadron claimed a further enemy aircraft destroyed, a Junkers Ju188, and there was further success two nights later when the squadron shot down a Ju188 to the west of Cherbourg followed the next night by five more successes for the squadron; three Ju188s and two FW190s were shot down before dawn had broken on 18 June. Then during the evening of 22 June, the Mitchells of No. 226 Squadron, followed by the two Boston squadrons at Hartford Bridge, took part in a successful bombing raid against a steel works at Caen where German defensive strong points had been holding up the advance of British troops on the ground for several days.

With the Allied forces safely ashore and now advancing further into Normandy, No. 141 Wing was disbanded when No. 322 Squadron left Hartford Bridge for West Malling to join No. 148 Wing in the continuous battle against the V-1 launch sites, followed by No. 264 Squadron's departure for Hunsdon to take part in anti-Diver patrols as an increasing number of

V-1 flying bombs were launched against London. By the time No. 264 Squadron left Hartford Bridge, Charles Ramsay had added two more successes to his total, both on the night of 4/5 July when he shot down a Junkers Ju88 and a Messerschmitt Me 410 over Normandy; Ramsay survived the war with at least seven confirmed kills for which he was awarded a bar to his DFC.

Hartford Bridge had received a number of important visitors during 1944, including a visit by King George VI and Queen Elizabeth in July when they visited the airfield to present a number of gallantry awards. The Hartford Bridge units were then involved in No. 2 Group's contribution to Operation *Market Garden* in September to support the airborne attempt to capture the strongly defended bridges at Nijmegen and Arnhem; the Mitchells of No. 226 Squadron were involved in daylight attacks in advance of the airborne forces.

As the number of Allied casualties in north-west Europe increased, Hartford Bridge, with its excellent road structure and close proximity to a number of hospitals in the area, was also used for receiving wounded soldiers back from the continent. By early October the Allies had advanced sufficiently far enough to allow the light-bombers of the 2nd TAF to cross the Channel. On 17 October No. 137 Wing left for Vitry en Artois (B.50) and Mosquitos of No. 138 Wing briefly moved in to Hartford Bridge from Lasham before the following month they, too, moved across the Channel to Cambrai/Epinoy (A.75). The 2nd TAF then formed a third Mosquito wing, No. 136 Wing, at Hartford Bridge following the arrival of No. 418 Squadron from Hunsdon and No. 605 Squadron from Manston but it would be some weeks before the wing had worked up sufficiently to take part in operations across the Channel.

On 2 December the airfield changed its name from Hartford Bridge to Blackbushe. By the end of the year the Mosquitos of No. 136 Wing were ready to commence operations and from then on were used to carry out a variety of attacks against German defences and units in the Ardennes, north-east Holland and north-west Germany. In March 1945 No. 136 Wing was the last 2nd TAF unit to cross the Channel into northern Europe but eventually, on 15 March 1945, the wing left Blackbushe for Coxyde in Belgium (B.71).

The Bushe Café provides great views of the former wartime airfield of Hartford Bridge.

With the departure of No. 136 Wing came the transfer of Blackbushe to No. 46 Group, Transport Command. A number of RAF units and commercial operators then operated from Blackbushe in the immediate aftermath of the war before the airfield closed as a military airfield in November 1946 but re-opened as Blackbushe Airport in February 1947 under the control of the Ministry of Civil Aviation. Its location close to London, combined with its existing road network, meant that Blackbushe was certainly attractive for commercial operations.

Blackbushe was used by a number of operators during the Berlin airlift of 1948 and the airfield then resumed its link with the RAF when it was used by transport aircraft of the Royal Auxiliary Air Force until 1953. Many commercial operators used Blackbushe during the late 1940s and 1950s but local opposition finally brought an end to Blackbushe Airport in May 1960. However, the legendary, and extremely influential, Air Vice-Marshal Donald Bennett, who had made his name during the war as the leader of the Pathfinder Force, had fought to maintain the existence of Blackbushe because the eastern part of the airfield had been developed on land that was privately owned. Bennett bought the land and the airfield was then re-opened in 1962 as a flying club and operator of executive aircraft. The hangars and former wartime buildings had, by then, been

Squadron	Dates at Hartford Bridge	Aircraft type
140 Squadron	13 Mar 43–7 Apr 44	Spitfire IV & XI/Blenheim IV/Ventura I/ Mosquito IX & XVI
16 Squadron	29 Jun 43–7 Apr 44	Mustang I/ Spitfire XI
21 Squadron	19 Aug–27 Sep 43	Ventura I/II
107 Squadron	1 Aug 43–3 Feb 44	Boston III
88 Squadron	19 Aug 43–17 Oct 44	Boston III/IV
342 (Free French) Squadron	6 Sep 43–17 Oct 44	Boston III/IV
226 Squadron	13 Feb–17 Oct 44	Mitchell II
322 (Dutch) Squadron	23 Apr–20 Jun 44	Spitfire XIV
264 Squadron	5 May–26 Jul 44	Mosquito XIII
107 Squadron	30 Oct–19 Nov 44	Mosquito VI
305 'Wielkopolski' Squadron	30 Oct–19 Nov 44	Mosquito VI
613 Squadron	30 Oct–19 Nov 44	Mosquito VI
418 Squadron RCAF	21 Nov 44–15 Mar 45	Mosquito VI
605 Squadron	21 Nov 44–15 Mar 45	Mosquito VI

removed, although the main runway and a second runway were considered suitable for use. The local opposition to the airfield did not go away and any requests for further development of the site resulted in planning permission being refused. Some years later Bennett sold the land to the millionaire Douglas Arnold.

Over the years Blackbushe has been used for a wide variety of events and activities. The wartime runway and original air traffic control tower were demolished in the 1960s. For many years Blackbushe was home to several historic aircraft from the Second World War but gradually these disappeared. A hangar and museum were erected on the south-western part of the airfield during the 1980s and the airfield used to straddle both sides of the A30 with traffic having to wait while aircraft were towed across the busy road. Today the part of the airfield

Typhoons of No. 121 Wing served at Holmsley South during the period of D-Day operations.

to the north of the A30 remains active and the airport is open to the public. The area is also very popular for walks around the perimeter of the airfield and to see the wildlife on Yateley Common.

The airport can be found from the M3 by exiting the motorway at Junction 4 and taking the A30 southbound towards Hook. You soon come to the airport and the entrance is on your right. You can park for free and observe the aircraft from this position and also get great views of the airfield from the Bushe Café, particularly from the patio area outside.

Holmsley South

This is a wonderful site to visit, not least because of its location in the heart of the New Forest; reminders of the former airfield of Holmsley South are still visible and it is the location of the most impressive New Forest Airfields memorial. Situated about 5 miles to the north-east of Christchurch, on the south-western edge of the New Forest and on the A35 towards Lyndhurst, this was another wartime airfield and was built during 1941–42 with the intention of providing accommodation for units of Coastal Command and for those supporting Operation *Torch*, the Anglo-American invasion of French North Africa in November 1942.

The airfield opened in September 1942 but it was some time before the technical buildings and accommodation were complete. However, the three runways and a few aircraft hardstandings were complete and No. 547 Squadron formed at Holmsley South on 21 October, although the squadron had yet to take delivery of the first of its Wellington aircraft; these would start to arrive the following month. The first operational aircraft to fly from the airfield were not Coastal Command aircraft but American B-24 Liberators attached to No. 19 Group, Coastal Command, tasked to carry out anti-submarine patrols in the Bay of Biscay. The elements of No. 547 Squadron did not stay long and by the end of the year they had moved out. Then for the first few months of 1943 Holmsley South was used by squadrons converting to the Halifax while the development of the airfield was completed. By the summer of 1943 the airfield was home to two Coastal Command squadrons carrying out anti-U-boat patrols in the Bay of Biscay and it remained that way until the end of the year when the squadrons moved out and early in 1944 Holmsley South was transferred to No. 10 Group, Fighter Command, for fighter operations.

The first 2nd TAF units to operate from the airfield were three Canadian squadrons – Nos 441, 442 and 443 Squadrons – which moved south from Digby in Lincolnshire and the first aircraft started to arrive on 18 March. Their purpose was to convert from the Spitfire V to the MkIX and to work up as No. 144 Wing, part of No. 83 Group, after which they would change places with No. 121 Wing at Westhampnett and take part in fighter sweeps across the Channel. The change-over happened on 1 April 1944 and the Typhoons of No. 121 Wing moved to Holmsley South where they would stay for the build-up to D-Day and beyond.

Commanding the airfield was Wing Commander C S Morice and now leading the Typhoons as Wing Commander Flying was Wing Commander Charles Green who had taken over command of the wing following the move from Westhampnett to Holmsley. Born in Southern Rhodesia, Green had joined the RAF before the outbreak of the Second World War and had initially flown with Coastal Command. By January 1942 he was flying Spitfires with No. 266 Squadron and was given command of the squadron until July 1943, during which time he was awarded the DFC. He later converted to the Typhoon and was given command of No. 121 Airfield in January 1944.

The Typhoons of Nos 174 and 175 Squadrons had already been equipped for rocket-firing missions and immediately began attacking key targets such as V-1 flying bomb sites, radar stations and communications targets in northern France. No. 245 Squadron had yet to convert and so its pilots and ground crew spent part of April and May at Eastchurch converting to its new capability before joining the other Holmsley squadrons on rocket-firing operations across the Channel.

By now the Typhoons had been joined at Holmsley South by another Canadian squadron, No. 418 Squadron, equipped with Mosquitos, which conducted intruder operations across the Channel. There was little flying during the two days before the Allied invasion as the Typhoons were prepared with the black and white invasion stripes to help prevent losses due to friendly fire but there were still losses just a matter of hours before the invasion when three Typhoons of the wing were lost during an attack against a radar site near Cap de la Hague. Despite the losses, the attack had been successful and had put the radar site out of action in time for the Allied invasion.

On D-Day Charles Green led No. 121 Wing in support of the first wave of troops as they went ashore at Omaha beach, carrying out rocket attacks against German gun batteries and other defensive positions overlooking the beach, a role the Typhoons continued throughout the D-Day period in direct support of the invading troops as they advanced into Normandy. Hitting the defensive positions was just one element of the fighter-bomber plan and an equally important task was to keep the German commanders on the ground in a state of confusion as to what was happening and where, and so the Typhoons were also used to carry out attacks against German headquarters and communications sites, as well as attacking other targets such as enemy airfields.

The Holmsley Typhoons enjoyed much success during the afternoon of 8 June when attacking a German airfield, which resulted in many enemy aircraft being destroyed on the ground. The following day the weather deteriorated, which resulted in a significant reduction in Allied sorties flown and at times brought air operations to a halt. Better weather saw operations resume and, the following day, ten rocket-armed Typhoons of No. 245 Squadron joined forces with thirty Typhoons of

No. 124 Wing at Hurn, and more than seventy Mitchells of No. 2 Group, to carry out a most successful attack against the headquarters of the commander of Panzer Group West, General Geyr von Schweppenburg, which was located in the Chateau de la Caine to the south-west of Caen. Poor weather had meant that the raid was delayed from the morning until early evening but the Typhoons, each armed with eight 60lb rockets, carried out a devastating attack resulting in the destruction of the headquarters, including vital communications and signals equipment, as well as the destruction of a number of vehicles located in the grounds of the chateau. So successful was the raid that it would be more than two weeks before the headquarters would be fully functional again.

During this period No. 174 Squadron was led by Squadron Leader Bill Pitt-Brown, who would soon be promoted and given command of No. 121 Wing, and leading No. 245 Squadron was Squadron Leader Jack Collins. During the late morning of 13 June the Typhoons flew across the Channel to the newly prepared landing strip at St Croix-sur-Mer (B.3); the idea was for the Typhoons to then conduct operations from across the Channel during the rest of the day before returning to Holmsley at dusk.

Within two weeks the Allied advance was sufficient to allow the first aircraft to cross the Channel and to operate from prepared strips in northern France. The Typhoons of No. 121 Wing were regularly crossing the Channel during the day to operate from Camilly (B.5) and then returning to Holmsley again until the airstrip became more habitable. The first Typhoons of No. 174 Squadron then left Holmsley on 19 June for Bazenville (B.2) and were amongst the first Allied aircraft to conduct operations from landing strips across the Channel, closely followed the day after by the Typhoons of No. 175 Squadron, which moved to St Croix-sur-Mer (B.3); the Typhoons of No. 245 Squadron would follow across the Channel the week after for Camilly (B.5) before moving on the next day to St André de l'Eure (B.24).

With the threat of the V-1 flying bomb against targets in southern England, No. 418 Squadron then concentrated on anti-Diver patrols and the squadron scored its first successes during mid-June. The departure of the Typhoon wing for northern France meant there was room for the arrival of No. 133

Wing from Coolham. The wing consisted of three squadrons of Mustangs – Nos 129, 306 and 315 Squadrons – which immediately commenced armed reconnaissance sorties from Holmsley. Leading the wing was the legendary Polish fighter ace, Wing Commander Stanislaw Skalski, who had escaped Europe in early 1940 and joined the RAF. Having served in the UK and North Africa, Skalski was given command of No. 601 Squadron in 1943; the first Pole to command an RAF squadron. He had assumed command of No. 133 Airfield in April 1944 and by the time he arrived at Holmsley South he had been credited with at least nineteen confirmed kills for which he had been awarded the DFC and two bars in addition to his extensive list of Polish awards.

Sadly, however, the wing did not get off to a good start at Holmsley and during the first afternoon of operations from the airfield the wing suffered four aircraft lost; two Mustangs each from Nos 129 and 315 Squadrons with two of the pilots killed. One of the pilots was Flight Lieutenant John Hancock of No. 129 Squadron. Following success in the Western Desert and Middle East, for which he had been awarded a DFC and bar, Hancock had joined the squadron in September 1943. Having been hit by flak, his aircraft crashed to the south-west of Thiberville.

It had not been a good day for the wing but the situation might well have been worse but for the quick-thinking commanding officer of No. 315 Squadron, Squadron Leader Eugeniusz Horbaczewski. Having already seen his flight commander, Flight Lieutenant Henryk Stefankiewicz, shot down by flak and crash into the sea near Cherbourg, killing the pilot, he then saw a second aircraft, flown by Warrant Officer Tadeusz Tamowicz, hit by flak and crash-land in marshland on the Cherbourg peninsula. Seeing an emergency landing ground still under construction nearby, Horbaczewski landed on the unfinished airstrip and commandeered an American jeep at the site and, with a handful of American engineers on board, he drove to the crashed Mustang where he then waded through the marshes to rescue his comrade. Horbaczewski then drove back to the airstrip where he put Tamowicz in the seat of his Mustang, then sat on his lap and flew the aircraft back to base with both men crammed inside the tiny cockpit. It was an extraordinary tale of quick thinking and bravery.

Eugeniusz Horbaczewski was, without doubt, one of the great Polish fighter pilots of the war. Born in Russia, he was twenty-six years old while serving at Holmsley. Like many other Poles he had escaped to France via Romania following the German invasion of Poland and had joined the RAF in 1940 and had then enjoyed much success flying Spitfires with the Desert Air Force and was particularly successful during the Tunisian campaign in 1943. By the time he took command of No. 315 Squadron in February 1944, Horbaczewski had been credited with eleven kills and he would add five more during the two months following the Allied invasion of Europe. Sadly, however, Eugeniusz Horbaczewski would be killed after leaving Holmsley South. On 18 August he led his squadron on a fighter sweep over the Beauvais area when the Mustangs encountered an estimated sixty Focke-Wulf FW190s around the airfield. During the next fifteen minutes, sixteen were claimed as shot down but, having shot down three FW190s himself, which brought his personal total to sixteen, Horbaczewski was shot down and killed.

This information board in the heart of the New Forest and situated just outside a camp site located on the former hardened aircraft dispersals marks the site of the former airfield of Holmsley South.

The New Forest Airfields Memorial was unveiled in 2002 and is situated on Black Lane and stands on the western edge of the former airfield.

On 23 June the Mustangs of No. 306 Squadron bombed a railway station at Verneuil after which they encountered a large mixed formation of Focke-Wulf FW190s and Messerschmitt Bf109s to the west of Dreux. It was around midday when the ferocious aerial combat took place, which resulted in the Mustang pilots shooting down seven enemy aircraft – four Bf109s and three FW190s – with four of the Mustangs also being shot down and one of the pilots, Squadron Leader Marciniak, killed. Two of the Bf109s were shot down near Verneuil by Flight Lieutenant Wladyslaw Potocki, bringing his total to five during the month for which he would be awarded the DFC. The following day, Stanislaw Skalski was also able to add to his total while leading the wing when, during his attack near Tilliers, his attack resulted in the collision of two Messerschmitt Bf109s. This took his total to at least twenty-one, and has been reported to be even higher, which made him the most successful Polish fighter pilot of the war.

It was not long before the squadrons moved to Ford, after which Holmsley South was handed over to the United States Ninth Air Force. It was then the turn of the Americans, once

The New Forest Airfields Memorial overlooks the site of the former airfield of Holmsley South.

more, to operate from the airfield with B-26 Marauders carrying out medium-level bombing raids over northern France. The Marauders moved across the Channel in September and the following month Holmsley South was transferred back to the RAF and allocated to Transport Command. In October 1946 the airfield was placed on care and maintenance and for many years parts of the airfield, including parts of the runway at the western side of the airfield, were privately owned with much of the former airfield being reclaimed by the Forestry Commission. The runways were removed during the 1960s and most of the site has since either reverted to heathland or has been used privately for farming.

Although most of the area has long reverted to heathland and farmland, the site of the former airfield is well worth a visit. The easiest way of finding the site is by travelling south-westwards along the A35 from Lyndhurst towards Christchurch. About 7 miles to the south-west of Lyndhurst, pass through the small village of Holmsley, remaining on the A35 towards Christchurch, and continue past the B3058 turning on your left towards the village of Wootton. You are now passing along the eastern

Remains of the former runway at Holmsley South can be found on Forest Road and mark the most western part of the runway that ran eastwards from this western part of the airfield.

boundary of the former airfield and just after the A35 bends left take the turning to the right, Lyndhurst Road, a minor road towards the village of Thorney Hill. After just a few hundred yards the road turns sharp right. This is Forest Road and you are now at the most southern part of the former airfield.

After a short distance of no more than 200 yards you will see farmland off to the right and you are now looking along the line of the runway that ran from the south-west part of the airfield, where you now are, to the north-east. Continuing along Forest Road, in a northerly direction towards the village of Thorney Hill, you are now following the line of the north-south runway. Turn left into Black Lane and follow the lane for a short distance until you come to the New Forest Airfields memorial, which stands on the western edge of the former airfield. The memorial, which was unveiled in 2002, came from the desire to commemorate all those who had served at airfields in the New Forest during the Second World War.

Returning back along Black Lane to Forest Road, turn left, northwards, and you will soon see on your left the tarmac of the runway that marks the most western part of the runway that ran from the west of the airfield to the east; the tarmac is on private land but you can park next to it to get a good view and to look across to the eastern part of the airfield and the line that the runway once took. If you then continue a few yards further along Forest Road you will see a turning to the right towards a campsite. You can follow this track down to the entrance of the campsite where a board has been erected to mark the site of the former airfield. The campsite is located on the former hardened aircraft dispersals that mark the northernmost point of the airfield.

Squadron	Dates at Holmsley South	Aircraft type
441 Squadron RCAF	18 Mar–1 Apr 44	Spitfire IX
442 Squadron RCAF	18 Mar–1 Apr 44	Spitfire IX
443 Squadron RCAF	18–27 Mar 44	Spitfire IX
174 Squadron	1 Apr–19 Jun 44	Typhoon I
175 Squadron	1 Apr–20 Jun 44	Typhoon I
245 Squadron	1 Apr–27 Jun 44	Typhoon I
418 Squadron RCAF	8 Apr–14 Jul 44	Mosquito VI
129 Squadron	22 Jun–9 Jul 44	Mustang III
306 'Torunski' Squadron	22–27 Jun 44	Mustang III
315 'Deblinski' Squadron	26 Jun 44	Mustang III

Ibsley

Situated 2 miles to the north of the town of Ringwood on the western edge of the New Forest, alongside the A338 towards Salisbury, is the village of Ibsley. Its airfield was home to Spitfires of the Czech Wing of the 2nd TAF during the winter of 1943–44 before it then became home to American fighters during the D-Day operations.

The airfield was constructed during late 1940 and early 1941 on the lower land bordering the county of Dorset as a satellite for Middle Wallop some 25 miles to the north-east. Ibsley opened in February 1941 and, like other airfields being developed in the area at the time, the first flying unit moved in before construction work was complete. The airfield would eventually have three hardened runways with two Bellman hangars and twelve Blister hangars around the site.

A memorial to RAF Ibsley, which also shows the layout of the former airfield, can be found at the crossroads at Cross Lanes in the village of Mockbeggar.

The first aircraft to operate from Ibsley were Hurricanes of No. 32 Squadron, which arrived from Middle Wallop on 16 February. The squadron was a veteran of the battles of France and Britain and was now tasked with providing night defence of southern England but the squadron moved out two months later and was replaced by Spitfires of No. 118 Squadron, which, for the next four months, carried out defensive patrols over southern England.

Development work continued throughout 1941 and by the end of the year Ibsley was home to a Spitfire wing led by Wing Commander Ian 'The Widge' Gleed, a veteran of the Battles of France and Britain, during which he had been credited with at least nine confirmed kills and had been awarded a DFC. For the next six months the wing provided fighter escort for bombers attacking targets across the Channel and Gleed was awarded a DSO for his leadership of the wing before he was posted to a staff appointment at HQ Fighter Command.

Ibsley was then handed over to the American Eighth Air Force during the summer of 1942 and the airfield was home to P-38

This smaller memorial to RAF Ibsley marks the end of the runway that ran from the south-eastwards part of the airfield towards the north-west and can be found on the right-hand side of Ellingham Drove when heading towards the main A338.

Lightnings. The American Fighter Group moved to the North African theatre at the end of the year and Ibsley was transferred to No. 10 Group, Fighter Command, but poor drainage meant that the airfield suffered from flooding during periods of heavy rain and this reduced the airfield's suitability to conduct operations. Improvements were then made to the airfield drainage facilities, and during the first half of 1943 Ibsley was home to a Spitfire wing – Nos 129, 504 and 616 Squadrons – which carried out a wide variety of operations across the Channel and northern France, such as providing fighter escort for American bombers carrying out daylight raids and the Spitfires also conducted low-level attacks against targets of convenience.

By September the squadrons had left and had been replaced by three more Spitfire squadrons – Nos 310, 312 and 313 Squadrons – of the Czech Wing. Now operating as No. 134 Airfield, part of No. 84 Group 2nd TAF, the Czech Wing provided fighter escort

Looking north across the gravel pits and the site of the former airfield of Ibsley.

for bombers over France and they were briefly joined at Ibsley at the end of the year by a fourth squadron, No. 263 Squadron, which was in the process of converting from the Whirlwind to the Typhoon. The squadron detached its pilots and ground crew to Fairwood Common and Beaulieu during January 1944 to conduct its conversion and training, and once complete the squadron resumed sweeps across the Channel in February before moving to Warmwell the following month.

By February 1944 the Czech Wing had moved out and Ibsley was, once again, home to the Americans and the first units of the US Ninth Air Force moved in. Throughout the build-up to the Allied invasion of Europe, and during the period of D-Day operations, Ibsley was used by the Americans and once landing strips were available across the Channel the American fighters left Ibsley. By the beginning of July they had all gone and Ibsley was then used for flying training and then, in March 1945, the airfield was transferred to Transport Command, as a satellite airfield for nearby Stoney Cross and Holmsley South, and was also used for gliding before Ibsley finally closed in 1947.

Like some other airfields, Ibsley was then used as a motor racing venue for a number of years. Managed by the Ringwood Motor Cycle and Light Car Club, the first event was held in 1951 and racing took part from the venue until the mid-1950s after which the land reverted to agriculture. During the 1960s the site was sold, the runways were removed and the former airfield was then quarried.

The site of the former airfield can be found by taking the A338 north of Ringwood towards Salisbury. The site is immediately to the east of the A338 just before you reach the village of Ibsley, with the southern boundary being marked by the minor road that links Ellingham and Rockford, called Ellingham Drove, and the northern boundary marked by the minor road that links the villages of Ibsley and Mockbeggar, called Mockbeggar Lane; the eastern boundary is marked by the minor lane connecting Mockbeggar and Moyles Court School. Although the former airfield is now under water as a result of quarrying, there are some reminders of the wartime airfield, although not all of them can be accessed by the public; the air traffic control tower, for example, is on private land. The RAF Ibsley Historical Group has done much over the years to preserve the legacy of this former airfield. In 2000 a granite commemorative plaque, resting on a

The former air traffic control tower can be seen from the minor road between the village of Mockbeggar and Moyles Court School, although it cannot be accessed by the public as it is on private land.

stone base, was unveiled to mark the role RAF Ibsley played during the Second World War.

You can view the site by following the minor roads around the former airfield. Take the A338 from Ringwood towards Salisbury and once you have passed the minor road that connects Ellingham and Rockford look to your right and you will see the lakes and gravel pits; this was the former airfield. But for now continue along the A338 and turn right at the village of Ibsley into Mockbeggar Lane towards Mockbeggar. After passing through the few houses you will see the site of the former airfield off to your right but continue until you come to the cross roads at Cross Lanes in the village of Mockbeggar, opposite the chapel, where on the right you will see the polished granite memorial to RAF Ibsley, which is situated on a concrete base where the old guardroom was located. If you turn right at the cross roads, now with the memorial on your immediate right, continue southwards towards Rockford. You will soon see Forelock Farm on your left and opposite is a gate and path leading down to the old air traffic control tower. If you stop here for a moment you can see the tower, although it is not fully in view and is not accessible to the public.

Then continue a short distance along the lane until you come to Moyles Court School on your right. Turn right there and head westwards along Ellingham Drove, back towards the A338. If you look carefully after a short distance you will see another, but much smaller, memorial to RAF Ibsley. This also marks the end of the runway that ran from the south-east of the airfield to the north-west. Soon after, and to the south of Ellingham Drove, is some old concrete marking the southern end of the north-south runway. Then continuing westwards along Ellingham Drove you pass through the Blashford Lakes Wildlife Reserve, an area of outstanding beauty and full of wildlife, and you will soon see a track on the right which then doubles back on itself. Turn along the track and without going on to private land you can get a good view from here across the lakes and gravel pits to the north and north-west. As you arrive back at the A338 you are in the south-west corner of the airfield. There are a few other buildings dispersed around the site. It was at Ibsley that the flying sequences from the classic wartime film *First of the Few*, starring David Niven and Leslie Howard, were filmed.

Squadron	Dates at Ibsley	Aircraft type
129 Squadron	13 Feb–28 Jun 43	Spitfire V / VI
504 Squadron	30 Dec 42–30 Jun 43	Spitfire V
616 Squadron	2 Jan–17 Sep 43	Spitfire VI
310 (Czech) Squadron	19 Sep 43–19 Feb 44	Spitfire V
312 (Czech) Squadron	21 Sep 43–19 Feb 44	Spitfire V
313 (Czech) Squadron	18 Sep 43–6 Jan 44	Spitfire V
263 Squadron	5 Dec 43–23 Jan 44	Typhoon I

Lasham

Situated about 4 miles to the north-west of the town of Alton and 5 miles to the south-east of Basingstoke, just to the east of the A339 connecting the two towns, the village of Lasham is set in the undulating countryside of northern Hampshire. The airfield is now the home of the Lasham Gliding Society and the aircraft maintenance company ATC Lasham but it was home to a Mosquito wing of No. 2 Group during 1944 and the D-Day operations.

Farmland in an area of dense woodland was identified in 1941 as a site for the potential development of an airfield and the plan was to use Lasham as a satellite for the bomber airfield at Aldermaston. Work soon began on the construction of three

Mitchells of No. 320 'Dutch' Squadron were based at Lasham during late 1943 and took part in a variety of operations including raids against enemy communications networks, enemy airfields and V-1 sites.

standard concrete runways, hardened aircraft dispersal areas and four hangars with a large technical site, together with permanent buildings around the site for accommodation.

When completed the main runway was 1,900 yards long and ran east–west with a second runway of 1,400 yards running from the south-west to the north-east and a third runway of 1,200 yards running north-south. Plans to use the airfield for bombers were cancelled and so the first to use Lasham was Army Co-Operation Command at the end of 1942. Initially the airfield was only used by ground units but flying commenced from Lasham in March 1943 as part of No. 124 Airfield. The first air force residents were Hurricane IIs of No. 175 Squadron and the Canadians of No. 412 Squadron, equipped with Spitfire Vs, but both squadrons only remained for a short time. They were replaced by the Spitfire Vs of No. 602 Squadron and Lasham then became home to a Typhoon wing. First to arrive was No. 181 Squadron in early April followed by Nos 182 and 183 Squadrons during the following month. Towards the end of May No. 175 Squadron arrived, to replace No. 183 Squadron, but a couple of weeks later the whole airfield moved to Appledram.

Lasham was then temporarily administered by No. 10 Group, Fighter Command and then No. 70 Group before it became part of No. 2 Group 2nd TAF at the end of August 1943. The first No. 2 Group unit to arrive was the Dutch No. 320 Squadron, equipped with Mitchell IIs, which arrived from Attlebridge. As part of the 2nd TAF, the squadron flew its first operational sorties from Lasham during September, initially against communications targets and from then on the squadron took part in raids against enemy airfields, railway yards and German defensive positions along the coastline of northern France, and towards the end of the year the Mitchells took part in attacks against the V-1 sites.

In October No. 613 Squadron arrived from Snailwell and immediately began converting from the Mustang I, which it had used for tactical reconnaissance and ground attack missions, to the Mosquito ready to commence fighter-bomber missions across the Channel. The Lasham squadrons became No. 138 Airfield and they were soon joined by the Polish unit, No. 305 'Weilkopolski' Squadron, a former Mitchell-equipped squadron from Swanton Morley but, after flying only a dozen or so operational sorties with the Mitchell, it had then been moved to Lasham to start its conversion to the Mosquito in preparation for carrying out low-level attacks against enemy airfields and transportation. The Lasham squadrons flew continuously during the winter months, mainly against enemy airfields and concentrations of transport vehicles, often running the gauntlet of ground fire and being threatened by enemy fighters while carrying out their attacks at low-level.

In February 1944 the Mitchells of No. 320 Squadron moved out and No. 107 Squadron moved in. The new squadron, which had previously operated Bostons from Hartford Bridge against enemy airfields, transportation and ports, now re-equipped with the Mosquito VI in preparation for conducting night intruder operations across the Channel. Lasham was now totally a Mosquito base and this is how things would remain throughout the summer of 1944. The Mosquitos were soon conducting operations across the Channel, taking part in a variety of raids but they mainly carried out attacks against the V-1 sites.

As the attention turned towards D-Day the Mosquitos, now operating as No. 138 Wing, were used more and more at night to carry out night intruder operations against communications targets in northern France as well as carrying out precision attacks against key targets by day, often operating with the Mosquitos of No. 140 Wing from Hunsdon.

Following the D-Day landings, the Mosquitos of No. 138 Wing at Lasham were often used to carry out precision raids against key enemy targets in Normandy.

Since the 1950s the former wartime airfield of Lasham has been much used for gliding and is now home to the Lasham Gliding Society, a centre of gliding excellence and the largest gliding club in the country. From here you can get the best view of the airfield.

One notable pilot operating from Lasham during this period was twenty-four-year-old Wing Commander Bob Braham. Although he was on a so-called 'rest tour' from operations at HQ No. 2 Group, where he had been serving as Wing Commander Night Operations since February 1944, Braham had scored his first success while flying Blenheims during the Battle of Britain and had then achieved much success as a night-fighter pilot flying Beaufighters with No. 29 Squadron and then with No. 141 Squadron. By the end of 1943 he had been credited with twenty kills and had been awarded a DFC and two bars and a DSO and bar.

Braham continued to fly from Lasham whenever he could, usually at least every week or two. Within days of taking up his appointment at HQ No. 2 Group he had flown a *Ranger* sortie with No. 613 Squadron and during more sorties with the squadron he had claimed three more successes during March and then a further three more successes while flying with No. 305 Squadron in April. On one *Ranger* across the North Sea to Denmark during the morning of 12 May, while again flying a Mosquito of No. 107 Squadron, Braham and his navigator, Flight

Aircraft maintenance of airliners and other executive aircraft requiring engineering overhauls is carried out by ATC Lasham at the western end of the airfield using a number of the original hangars and buildings.

Lieutenant 'Sticks' Gregory had destroyed a Focke-Wulf FW190 near Aalborg before they were then attacked by a Messerschmitt Bf109 and they were also hit by flak. Braham did his best to get the Mosquito back to an airfield but he eventually had to make a forced-landing into the sea off the Norfolk coastline but, fortunately, the crew had come down close to some friendly Royal Navy ships and were rescued. Braham was then grounded, for the next few weeks at least. His success on 12 May was his twenty-ninth kill and a second bar to his DSO followed. Braham would later resume operations after D-Day but he was shot down on 25 June while flying with No. 21 Squadron and taken as a prisoner of war.

During the period of D-Day operations, together with other Mosquitos, the Lasham-based squadrons maintained a patrol over the Normandy area and during the daylight hours carried out attacks against road and rail junctions to disrupt German attempts to reinforce the area; this continued throughout the period until the Allies were able to break out of the Normandy area.

During the early hours of 8 June the Mosquito fighter-bombers from Nos 107 and 305 Squadrons were instructed to carry out

A memorial to RAF Lasham can be found at the entrance to the gliding club, which is off the minor road known as the Avenue that connects the A339 and B3349.

attacks against German army units in the Mézidon and Carentan area that were attempting to get forward to the invasion area as reinforcements; each squadron lost one aircraft with both crews killed. The weather then deteriorated on 9 June, which resulted in a significant reduction in Allied sorties flown and at times brought air operations to a halt. Better weather saw operations soon resume and the operational tempo from Lasham was extremely high during the immediate aftermath of D-Day with No. 138 Wing flying well over 2,000 sorties from Lasham during the following three months.

No. 305 Squadron suffered a significant loss during the morning of 16 June when Squadron Leader Mike Herrick was shot down and killed, with his radar operator, Flying Officer Turski, during a *Ranger* sortie to the Danish coast. Herrick had been flying as a pair with Bob Braham when the Mosquitos were attacked by a Focke-Wulf FW190 over the North Sea. The young New Zealander, Mike Herrick, was already an accomplished ace having been the first successful night-fighter pilot, claiming three victories while flying Blenheims with No. 25 Squadron during the Battle of Britain, two of which were in one night, for which he was awarded the DFC. He later flew Beaufighters with the same squadron and then Kittyhawks with the RNZAF, adding more successes and a bar to his DFC, before he was posted to Lasham as a flight commander with No. 305 Squadron. At the time of his death Mike Herrick was just twenty-three years old. He was the youngest of six brothers, with all six seeing active service during the war, although, sadly, three of them were killed serving with the RAF.

The Mosquito VI proved to be an excellent aircraft for carrying out precision attacks and during the summer of 1944 the wing, usually operating in relatively small numbers of five or six aircraft, took part in a number of raids against specific targets such as chateaux or other buildings in northern France that were being used as headquarters, for housing troops or for other key purposes. During September the Lasham squadrons supported Operation *Market* to provide vital air support to the Allied troops in and around Arnhem. The Mosquito crews dropped 500lb bombs but this proved extremely hazardous because attacks against German positions in the town had to be made at very low-level and in the face of heavy flak. The Mosquitos did score some success but they also suffered losses and the eventual outcome at Arnhem proved costly for the Allies.

One of the original wartime buildings can be seen from the Avenue.

An aerial view of Lasham looking south and clearly showing the main runway, which is now used by ATC Lasham for airliners and other executive aircraft requiring engineering maintenance. The maintenance hangars and buildings used by ATC can be seen on the right, at the western end of the airfield, and the gliding club facilities run along the bottom of the photo and mark the northern edge of the airfield. (Robert Pollett)

At the end of October No. 138 Wing moved to Hartford Bridge before soon crossing the Channel to Cambrai/Epinoy (A.75) to conduct operations from northern France. For the next month Lasham was quiet until the arrival of No. 84 Group Support Unit, which moved in from Thruxton with the task of providing replacement aircraft and crews to the operational squadrons. Lasham was then transferred to No. 11 Group as a satellite airfield for nearby Blackbushe. In the immediate aftermath of the Second World War the airfield was used by various maintenance units until Lasham closed towards the end of 1948, although the airfield was retained by Fighter Command.

During the 1950s and 1960s there was a large aircraft scrap yard at Lasham, which was operated by Staravia and contained dozens of old aircraft, mostly military, in the hangars and dispersal area to the north of the airfield. From the 1950s Lasham was also home to much gliding and in 1961 the airfield was transferred from the Air Ministry to the Ministry of Aviation. The Lasham Gliding Centre has since become a centre of gliding excellence and popularity, and in 1999 the society bought the freehold of the airfield from the Ministry of Defence.

Today there is one main runway that runs east–west, which is used by business and executive jets, with the Lasham Gliding Society using the grass to the north of the runway. Aircraft maintenance is carried out by ATC Lasham at the western end of the airfield using a number of the airfield's original hangars and buildings, and the company uses the main runway to bring in airliners and other executive aircraft for engineering overhauls. The gliding club, which has occupied the airfield since it was vacated by the RAF in the 1950s, is now the largest in the country and offers a wide range of training.

Lasham is worth a visit but it is not possible to gain general access to the airfield. It can be found by taking the A339 from Alton towards Basingstoke or from the B3349 road towards Hook. The best place to view the airfield is from the gliding club, preferably with prior permission to enter the facility. The entrance to the glider club is on the southern side of the minor road, known as the Avenue, which runs east-west and connects the A339 and B3349. There was once a museum adjacent to the gliding club but this is no longer there, although there is a memorial to RAF Lasham at the entrance.

Squadron	Dates at Lasham	Aircraft type
175 Squadron	11–13 Mar 43	Hurricane II
412 Squadron RCAF	7 Mar–8 Apr 43	Spitfire V
602 Squadron	14–29 Apr 43	Spitfire V
181 Squadron	5 Apr–2 Jun 43	Typhoon I
182 Squadron	29 Apr–2 Jun 43	Typhoon I
183 Squadron	3–30 May 43	Typhoon I
175 Squadron	24 May–2 Jun 43	Typhoon I
320 (Dutch) Squadron	30 Aug 43–18 Feb 44	Mitchell II
613 Squadron	12 Oct 43–30 Oct 44	Mosquito VI
305 'Wielkopolski' Squadron	18 Nov 43–30 Oct 44	Mosquito VI
107 Squadron	3 Feb–30 Oct 44	Mosquito VI

Lee-on-Solent

About 3 miles to the north-west of Gosport, where Southampton Water meets the Solent, is the town of Lee-on-Solent. The airfield is just to the north of the town and is still active today but this former naval base was used by Spitfires of the 2nd TAF as part of an Air Spotting Pool that provided vital bombardment spotting for the naval forces supporting the D-Day landings.

Its origins date back to 1917 when Lee-on-Solent was developed for the Royal Naval Air Service. Having been transferred to the Air Ministry in 1918, Lee-on-Solent was then retained in the post-war era and was used as a sea plane and float plane training base during the 1920s and 1930s. The airfield was originally grass with three runways. The main runway of 1,400 yards ran from the south-west to the north-east, the second runway of 1,100 yards ran from east–west and the shortest runway of 950 yards ran from north-south. A slipway to the south of the airfield was used for sea planes.

The airfield was then transferred to the Admiralty as HMS *Daedalus* in 1939. Although the Luftwaffe might have thought that Lee-on-Solent was being used by Fighter Command during the Battle of Britain, it was not but that did not stop the Luftwaffe bombing the airfield during August 1940, which resulted in significant damage including the destruction of three hangars and several aircraft on the ground.

Following military cutbacks naval flying ceased from Lee-on-Solent in 1988 but the airfield, now owned by the Department of Transport, can be seen when travelling along the B3385 southwards towards the town.

Looking across the former wartime airfield of Lee-on-Solent, which is now used for general aviation and gliding as well as being used by the Coastguard and Hampshire Constabulary.

During the following two years Lee-on-Solent was used by a number of Fleet Air Arm units as the airfield was improved in 1942 when tarmac was laid for the runways. There was a perimeter track laid and a number of aircraft blast pens constructed around the track. More land was then acquired at the eastern side of the airfield, which allowed significant improvements; the main runway was extended to 1,500 yards in length, the second runway was aligned more towards an east-west direction, a third runway of 1,000 yards was constructed in a north–south direction, more aircraft dispersals were built on the eastern side of the airfield and more hangars were constructed.

By the early months of 1944 Lee-on-Solent had an increased commitment to support the forthcoming Allied invasion of Europe. Some squadrons became part of the 2nd TAF while others formed naval fighter wings. A wing of Seafires (a naval version of the Spitfire) – No. 3 Naval Fighter Wing – had already arrived and the first RAF squadron, No. 26 Squadron, equipped with Spitfire Vs, arrived at the end of April. The Seafires and Spitfires took part in training with naval units for bombardment spotting for naval guns, a task they would carry out on D-Day.

A week before D-Day a second Spitfire squadron, No. 63 Squadron, arrived from Woodvale to join No. 26 Squadron and the two squadrons, together with the Seafires and aircraft of the United States Navy, were part of an Air Spotting Pool, known as No. 34 Recce Wing 2nd TAF, which provided vital air spotting for the naval forces supporting the Allied landings; a total of two RAF Spitfire V squadrons plus one flight of Typhoon Is, four Fleet Air Arm squadrons (Nos 808, 885, 886 and 897 Squadrons) with Seafires and Spitfire Vs, and a US Navy unit (VCS-7) also equipped with Spitfire Vs.

The wing was airborne before first light on D-Day and once it was light the pilots soon began to identify targets for the naval guns of the supporting ships. This was a most hazardous operation and the wing suffered its first loss while supporting the first wave when a Spitfire V was shot down to the east of the Cherbourg peninsula. More than 300 sorties were flown by the air spotters on D-Day, although the wing lost five aircraft during the day; three Spitfires and two Seafires with the loss of two pilots killed.

The Air Spotting Pool continued to suffer the following day, 7 June. During the early afternoon, a Spitfire of No. 26 Squadron was shot down by flak and crashed near Bayeux; twenty-one- year-old Flying Officer Ronald Wilcock was killed. Also, three naval Seafires of No. 886 Squadron were brought down with two of the aircraft having to make crash-landings in Normandy but all of the pilots were safe, two aircraft of No. 808 Squadron, one Spitfire and one Seafire, were shot down by Messerschmitt Bf109s but both pilots survived, and a Seafire of No. 885 Squadron was also lost, although the pilot survived. Amongst all the losses, however, there was also success with a Seafire of No. 886 Squadron shooting down a Messerschmitt Bf109 to the south of Evrecy.

Air spotting proved to be hazardous for the pilots and at least one Spitfire from No. 63 Squadron is thought to have been lost to anti-aircraft fire from Allied warships, although in this case, on 8 June, the pilot managed to bale out and later return to his unit. On the same day, however, the Royal Navy Seafire pilots did enjoy some success against enemy fighters and two pilots made claims against Focke-Wulf FW190s during the day.

The weather then deteriorated on 9 June, which resulted in a significant reduction in Allied sorties flown and at times brought air operations to a halt. An improvement in the weather soon saw operations resume and it was much the same during the following days whenever the weather permitted. Lee-on-Solent was one of the busiest 2nd TAF air bases. By the end of June, as the Allies increased their foothold in Normandy, there was less and less need for air spotting for the naval guns and No. 63 Squadron left Lee-on-Solent for Ballyherbert, although the squadron would later return to Lee-on-Solent at the end of August. The two squadrons then resumed working together until No. 63 Squadron left for the last time in mid-September and No. 26 Squadron left at the beginning of October. Lee-on-Solent was then an all-navy airfield once more.

Lee-on-Solent remained an active airfield for the Fleet Air Arm long after the Second World War was over and was re-named HMS *Ariel* in 1959, to reflect the emphasis on electrical and radar training, and then HMS *Daedalus* in 1965. Throughout the 1970s and 1980s the main role of the station was as a training base but the airfield was also home to many aircraft involved in a variety of tasks such as fishery protection, VIP transportation and to provide search and rescue coverage in the area. Following military cutbacks, naval flying ceased in 1988 when it was decided there was no longer the need for the airfield and HMS *Daedalus* finally closed in 1996.

The airfield was then used by the Royal Navy Gliding Club and the Police Air Wing, and occasionally by light aircraft. There were various proposals to turn the airfield into a main airfield for general aviation in the south of England due to the ever-increasing demands on nearby Southampton airport. In 2006 the site was split with ownership of the runways and the central area of the airfield transferred to the Maritime and Coastguard Agency with the surrounding areas being transferred to the South East England Development Agency. The airfield is now owned by the Department of Transport and is used for general aviation purposes, including gliding, and by the Coastguard and Hampshire Constabulary. It was announced in 2010 that the aircraft company Britten-Norman was moving production of its Defender aircraft to a new facility at Lee-on-Solent and the following year the company signed a two-year lease, which will allow continued operation of the airfield.

Only one hardened runway remains in use today, which runs from the south-west of the site to the north-east, with gliders operating from the grass parallel to the main runway. The site is easy to find by following the B3385 southwards from Fareham towards Lee-on-Solent. After crossing the junction with the B3334, the road is named Broom Way and the airfield can easily be seen on your right. The entrance to the site can be found by taking the first turning right, although prior permission to enter the site is required.

Squadron	Dates at Lee-on-Solent	Aircraft type
26 Squadron	28 Apr–6 Oct 44	Spitfire V
63 Squadron	28 May–3 Jul 44	Spitfire V
	30 Aug–19 Sep 44	Spitfire V

Needs Oar Point

This beautiful location on the southern edge of the New Forest, where the New Forest meets the Solent and overlooking the Isle of Wight at the mouth of the Beaulieu River, was once the site of an advanced landing ground and home to four Typhoon squadrons during the D-Day operations in June 1944.

Needs Oar Point was one of many sites identified during 1942 for development as an ALG and, being relatively small, it was only ever intended that the airfield facilities would be basic, with tents for accommodation and only basic aircraft servicing carried out on site. Work began the following spring with Sommerfeld track runways laid in preparation for the first Typhoons of No. 146 Airfield, No. 84 Group, to arrive.

The first of the Typhoons arrived from Tangmere on 10 April 1944 and within two days Needs Oar Point was suddenly home to four squadrons; a total of 120 aircraft. No. 146 Airfield was led by Wing Commander E W W Ellis and appointed as Wing Commander Flying was Wing Commander Reg Baker, a successful Whirlwind pilot and the last commander of a Whirlwind squadron before he was appointed as the wing leader at Harrowbeer prior to his posting to No. 146 Airfield. It was not long before the Typhoons were in action across the Channel. Carrying 500lb bombs, their targets included communications

Typhoons of No. 197 Squadron operated from Needs Oar Point as part of No. 146 Wing on D-Day.

targets in northern France, such as railway junctions and tunnels, enemy transport and troop concentrations, and other key targets such as radar sites. One of the largest *Ramrods* was flown on 26 April when Wing Commander Denys Gillam led two squadrons of Typhoons from Needs Oar Point, Nos 197 and 257 Squadrons, plus two more squadrons of Typhoons from Thorney Island, led by Wing Commander Billy Drake, on a low-level attack against a V-1 site. The raid was a great success, without any Typhoon losses, and this raid marked the first of a number of large-scale efforts by the Typhoon squadrons against specific targets of key importance.

The bomb-carrying Typhoons of No. 146 Airfield were then given a secondary role of smoke-laying, using smoke canisters under each wing, and during April and May the pilots carried out a number of exercises with the Army, although the wing never carried out this role operationally. On 18 May the airfield received a visit from the Prime Minister of Southern Rhodesia when the Prime Minister presented a new Typhoon aircraft to No. 266 (Rhodesia) Squadron. The airfield was now involved with the final build-up to D-Day, although one of the squadrons, No. 193 Squadron, suffered a loss just a matter of hours before the Allied invasion when its commanding officer, Squadron Leader D G Ross, was killed during the early morning of 5 June.

There had not been much flying that day, or the previous day, as the Typhoons were now being prepared with the black and white invasion stripes to help prevent losses from friendly fire and they were now operating as No. 146 Wing, with more than 150 aircraft available.

The Typhoons were heavily involved on D-Day and the wing was tasked with attacking a tank concentration area near Bayeux and also to fly sorties known as 'cab rank' sorties where the Typhoons, usually operating in pairs, would loiter over the invasion area from where they could be called in by an army controller on the ground to attack any target in support of the troops on the beachhead or during their advance beyond.

Each pilot would have his own tale to tell about his involvement on D-Day. For some it was reasonably straightforward in that he took off from Needs Oar Point and later landed back at the airfield without much incident. For others, however, the day turned out to be quite different to what they might have imagined at first light. One example was the experience of Sergeant Edward Donne. At around 5.00 p.m., he took off from Needs Oar Point with eight other Typhoons of No. 266 Squadron to carry out an armed reconnaissance sortie to look for tanks in the area to the south-east of Caen. Once the Typhoons were about 15 miles to the south of Caen the pilots spotted a column of German transport and immediately carried out a bombing attack. Like the other pilots, Donne dropped his bomb but the intense explosion caused his aircraft to rise suddenly and as he turned for home he checked his aircraft and engine for signs of damage. Realising that damage to his engine was going to prevent him from making it back across the Channel, Donne had no alternative but to bale out. He came down in a field just to the south-west of Caen and hid his parachute, Mae West and gauntlets in a hedge and then ran northwards away from where he might have been seen to have come down. Once clear of the area Donne hid between the hedges until it was dark but he enjoyed a commanding view of German tanks heading south and watched an attack by Allied aircraft against a nearby wood. Donne later continued his journey northwards and tried to elicit help from some local French civilians who refused to get involved. He finally came across some Allied Sherman tanks and he soon caught a lift by motorcycle to the headquarters area,

Typhoons and personnel of No. 266 'Rhodesia' Squadron, which arrived at Needs Oar Point in April 1944, and one of four Typhoon squadrons that made up No. 146 Wing.

from where he was taken by jeep to the beachhead and he then left Normandy by landing craft the following night.

The Typhoons enjoyed much success on D-day and in the immediate days after but there were also losses. One example was during the afternoon of 8 June when No. 266 Squadron was operating over the invasion area in support of the troops on the ground. The Typhoons were carrying out attacks against enemy vehicles near Caen when they were attacked by Messerschmitt Bf109s; one aircraft, flown by Flying Officer H C Ballance, was hit. Ballance immediately turned for home but was unable to make it all the way back across the Channel and ended up having to bale out of his aircraft before fortunately being rescued.

The weather then deteriorated on 9 June, which resulted in a significant reduction in Allied sorties flown and at times brought air operations to a halt. However, better weather soon saw operations resume but, sadly, No. 257 Squadron lost its commanding officer, Squadron Leader Ronnie Fokes, during the late morning of 12 June when he was shot down by flak to the south of Caen. His loss was significant for the squadron and for the airfield. Fokes had flown Spitfires as a sergeant pilot with No. 92 Squadron during 1940. Having claimed his first success over the Dunkirk beaches in early June, and then adding to his total during the Battle of Britain, Fokes was awarded a DFM

Commanding No. 146 Wing at Needs Oar Point during June 1944 was Wing Commander Johnny Baldwin, the top-scoring Typhoon pilot; his twelve victories had all been achieved while flying the Typhoon. Baldwin would add three more victories to his total during the following month and would later be awarded a bar to his DSO; he already had a DFC and bar.

before being commissioned at the end of the year having achieved nine victories. In March 1944 he was awarded a DFC having also been promoted and given command of No. 257 Squadron. Fokes was due to hand over command of the squadron before the Allied invasion of Europe but had asked instead to remain in command to see the squadron through the D-Day period; his request was granted but, sadly, it was a decision that would cost him his life.

The airfield of Needs Oar Point suffered a further devastating loss on 16 June during a midday sortie over Normandy when the popular and charismatic leader of No. 146 Wing, Reg Baker, was shot down by flak to the west of Caen. Operations were then brought to a temporary halt when, completely unexpectedly, a strong gale blew up in the Channel during the early hours of 19 June. However, by the 22 June the weather had cleared for operations to resume. Once the Allied troops started to break out of Normandy the Typhoons reverted to their previous task of low-level rocket and bombing attacks against key targets.

Command of No. 146 Wing had now passed to Wing Commander Johnny Baldwin, a former squadron commander of No. 198 Squadron and the top-scoring Typhoon pilot. There were none who knew the Typhoon better than Baldwin. However, he had been a relatively late starter as a pilot as far as his rise amongst the ranks was concerned. Baldwin had joined the RAFVR as ground crew at the outbreak of the Second World War and served in France with the British Expeditionary

Force and then on bomb disposal duties during the Blitz. He then volunteered for pilot training in 1941 and after training in the United States, Johnny Baldwin had flown Typhoons since completion of his training. His promotion had been rapid. By the time he was given command of No. 146 Wing at Needs Oar Point, and just eighteen months after he had completed pilot training, he had twelve confirmed kills to his name and he had been awarded a DFC and bar and a DSO for his leadership of No. 198 Squadron.

On 27 June Baldwin led the four squadrons of the wing in a coordinated attack with Mitchells of No. 2 Group against a farmhouse being used as the headquarters of the German general, *Generalleutnant* Dohlmann. The raid was highly successful and resulted in the farmhouse being totally destroyed with Dohlmann killed during the attack. There was further success for the wing just two days later, during the late morning of 29 June, when Baldwin led ten Typhoons of No. 193 Squadron tasked with escorting Typhoons of No. 183 Squadron from Hurn. The mission was to attack a railway marshalling yard and it was near to the airfield at Conches that the Typhoons encountered a large formation of Messerschmitt Bf109s and a fierce dogfight commenced. During the following air combat the Typhoons of No. 193 Squadron shot down five Bf109s, two of which were credited to Baldwin, his thirteenth and fourteenth successes of the war, with damage to at least five more; no Typhoons were lost.

By the beginning of July the four squadrons had all left Needs Oar Point, initially for Hurn before crossing the Channel two weeks later to operate from landing strips in northern France; they had been at Needs Oar Point for less than two months. By the end of 1944 work had started to return the site back to its pre-airfield days and much of the land had already reverted to farming by the end of the war.

Today there is very little evidence of the former airfield but the site can be found to the south of Bucklers Hard near Beaulieu. If travelling from the Lymington direction, travel eastwards from East End along St Leonards Road. Just before St Leonards you will pass a turn off to Park Farm, which was used during the war as the Officers' Mess. The road leading down to the farm, called Park Lane, is a private track but only a matter of yards

The site of the former wartime airfield of Needs Oar Point, which is set in a beautiful location where the New Forest meets the Solent and overlooking the Isle of Wight at the mouth of the Beaulieu River.

later, having continued along St Leonards Road, you will see on your right a board marking the site of the former airfield. This is the best place to stop and look south across the site of the former airfield and you also get a marvellous view across the Solent to the Isle of Wight.

Squadron	Dates at Needs Oar Point	Aircraft type
193 Squadron	11 Apr–3 Jul 44	Typhoon I
197 Squadron	10 Apr–3 Jul 44	Typhoon I
257 Squadron	10 Apr–2 Jul 44	Typhoon I
266 Squadron	10 Apr–29 Jun 44	Typhoon I

Odiham

Situated in the northern part of Hampshire, approximately midway between Basingstoke and Aldershot, and to the south of the A287, RAF Odiham is now home to the Chinook helicopter force and is known to most for supporting recent operations in Iraq and Afghanistan. But it was once a key airfield of the 2nd

A Mustang of No. 2 Squadron pictured at Odiham during 1943. This tactical reconnaissance squadron left Odiham in early 1944 but returned soon after D-Day as part of No. 35 (Recce) Wing.

TAF during 1943–44 and home to a photo-reconnaissance wing of Mustangs and Spitfires.

The origins of the airfield date back to the mid-1920s when the site was identified by the Air Ministry as a suitable landing ground for exercises and summer camps because of its close proximity to Aldershot and the established airfields nearby at Farnborough and Andover. The RAF's Expansion Scheme of the 1930s meant that more airfields were needed and so Odiham was an obvious choice for further development. More land was purchased and work began during the mid-1930s to extend and develop the airfield so that Odiham was capable of accommodating three Army Co-Operation squadrons. By the end of 1936 the airfield was finished with three large hangars and many technical and domestic accommodation buildings. The first squadrons moved in during early 1937 but drainage problems had caused some concern and so concrete runways were laid during 1939.

The opening months of the Second World War saw the Odiham squadrons, equipped with Hectors and Lysanders, exercising regularly with the Army. After the fall of France Odiham was

A visiting Typhoon at Odiham soon after D-Day.

home to the first element of the Free French training squadron, equipped with various surviving French aircraft and pilots that had escaped from France. The airfield occasionally became the attention of the Luftwaffe during the summer of 1940 and again during early 1941 but little damage occurred and the runways remained completely intact. More development work took place during 1941, including the construction of a perimeter track and aircraft hardstandings in front of the main hangars, and more land was purchased to extend the runways resulting in the main runway, which ran east–west, becoming 1,700 yards long and the second runway, running from the south-west to north-east, became 1,400 yards long; the third runway, which ran from the south-east to the north-west at the time, would no longer be used.

By the summer of 1942 the airfield was home to Army Co-Operation Blenheims, Tomahawks and Mustangs, and a year later Odiham had been transferred to Fighter Command and was now home to four Mustang squadrons of No. 123 Airfield, which were conducting tactical reconnaissance sorties over northern France. During August the number of Mustang squadrons increased to five, meaning that all the available space was being used, but by November 1943 there were just two resident units – Nos 2 and 4 Squadrons – designated No. 130 Airfield, part of No. 84 Group 2nd TAF.

The departure of the last Mustangs during early 1944 marked a change in aircraft and a change in role for Odiham from that of tactical reconnaissance to photo-reconnaissance. No. 400 Squadron arrived in February and converted from the Mustang I to the Spitfire XI and Mosquito XVI as a photographic unit for the preparation of the Allied invasion of Europe. The airfield was also visited by other 2nd TAF aircraft, mainly Typhoons, during early 1944, including a detachment of Typhoons from Nos 181 and 247 Squadrons, which deployed to Odiham from Merston in West Sussex during the first two weeks of the year to carry out attacks against emerging V-1 flying bomb sites in northern France. Odiham was also home to a forward repair unit with its personnel working on a variety of aircraft in preparation for the Allied invasion.

At the beginning of April three tactical reconnaissance Mustang squadrons – Nos 168, 414 and 430 Squadrons – of No. 128 Airfield, No. 83 Group, moved in to Odiham from Gatwick. Once again, space was at a premium at Odiham with three different aircraft types operating together from the airfield – Spitfires, Typhoons and Mustangs – with the personnel from the Mustang squadrons accommodated in tents in villages nearby. No. 128 Airfield was then designated No. 128 Wing in May and it would be these three Mustang squadrons, plus the Spitfires of No. 400 Squadron, that would operate from Odiham together as No. 39 (Photo Reconnaissance) Wing during the final build-up to D-Day and then during the days beyond.

Bad weather at the beginning of June grounded most of the Odiham aircraft for a while but the weather had improved by 6 June to support the Allied invasion of Europe. On D-Day the wing was heavily involved from first light. The Mustangs of No. 414 Squadron joined other air spotting aircraft operating over the invasion area to help direct fire from the armada of naval warships positioned off the landing beaches, one of the most hazardous operations during the day, while Odiham's other tactical reconnaissance Mustangs flew continuously over the invasion area, some 100 sorties during the day, which also included attacks against enemy defensive positions as the Allied troops went ashore.

The wing suffered one of the first casualties to enemy fighters during the afternoon of 6 June. Three Mustangs of No. 430 Squadron, led by Wing Commander Godfrey, commanding No. 128 Wing, were carrying out a reconnaissance sortie in the Montfort-Evreux area during the late afternoon when they were attacked by six Focke-Wulf FW190s. Godfrey and another Mustang, flown by Squadron Leader Chesters, managed to escape but the young Canadian Flying Officer Jack Cox was shot down to the north-east of Bernay and killed; Cox was twenty-three years old and is buried in the Bretteville-sur-Laize Canadian war cemetery to the south of Caen.

During the early morning of the following day, 7 June, two Mustangs of No. 414 Squadron were carrying out a tactical reconnaissance sortie to the north of Martagne at 6.30 a.m. when they spotted a Junkers Ju52 transport aircraft. The two Mustang pilots made the most of the opportunity and shot down the Ju52; it was the first Allied success of the day. One of the successful pilots was Flying Officer Roger Bromley but sadly he would not survive the Allied offensive and was killed while operating from Odiham soon after, on 18 June, when he failed to return from a sortie over the invasion area. Odiham suffered a further loss on 8 June when Mustangs of No. 168 Squadron were carrying out a tactical reconnaissance sortie to the east of Argentan when they were attacked by a dozen Focke-Wulf FW190s; one aircraft flown by Flying Officer J J Low was shot down and the pilot killed.

The weather then deteriorated on 9 June, which resulted in a significant reduction in Allied sorties flown and at times brought air operations to a halt. Better weather saw operations soon resume and the following afternoon two Mustangs of No. 414 Squadron were operating across the Channel and taking photographs of enemy gun positions near to the advancing Allied troops when they were attacked by eight Focke-Wulf FW190s to the north of Mézidon. Fortunately, Spitfire IXs in the area had seen the encounter and both Mustangs managed to escape after one of the Mustang pilots had managed to inflict damage to one of the FW190s.

Whenever the weather permitted it was much the same during the following days as the Odiham squadrons continued to provide vital support to the Allied invasion. However, the

The former wartime air traffic control tower at Odiham, which can only be seen by prior arrangement when visiting the RAF station today.

extremely hazardous nature of tactical reconnaissance meant there were losses; for example during the late afternoon on 18 June when a pair of Mustangs of No. 414 Squadron failed to return from a reconnaissance sortie in the Le Beny Bocage area. The Mustangs had been attacked by Focke-Wulf FW190s and both pilots – Flight Lieutenant J A MacKelvie and Flying Officer R A Bromley – were killed.

Completely unexpectedly, a strong gale blew up in the Channel during the early hours of 19 June, which brought daylight operations to a standstill for the following three days. However, by the 22 June the weather had cleared for operations to resume. Then, on 29 June, the Mustangs of Nos 168 and 430 Squadrons crossed the Channel to operate from the landing strip at Sommervieu (B.8), followed two days later by the Spitfires of No. 400 Squadron, leaving just No. 414 Squadron at Odiham; this squadron would cross the Channel on 15 August to operate from St Honorine (B.21).

Replacing No. 39 (Photo Reconnaissance) Wing was No. 35 (Reconnaissance) Wing of No. 84 Group, previously numbered

Now home to the Chinook helicopter, which requires no introduction because of its recent operations in Iraq and Afghanistan, Odiham is still a main operating base for the RAF.

No. 130 Wing and also equipped with Mustangs and Spitfires, which moved into Odiham from Gatwick. The tactical reconnaissance Mustangs, in particular, continued to play a vital role over Normandy; specifically to seek out key targets or troop concentrations and reinforcements. By the middle of August the three squadrons had left Odiham to cross the Channel. The forward repair unit also left for the continent and the sky over Odiham village suddenly fell quiet. The airfield was then briefly home to Mosquitos of No. 96 Squadron, which carried out anti-Diver patrols against the V-1 flying bombs targeted against southern England, and at the end of the year Odiham was home to two Mosquito night-fighter squadrons (Nos 264 and 604 Squadrons) of No. 147 Wing.

Odiham was now quiet and remained so until the end of the war when the airfield was used for the repatriation of prisoners of war, after which the airfield was transferred to Transport Command and then later in the year to the Royal Canadian Air Force. However, this was short-lived and during 1946 Odiham was transferred back to the RAF as an airfield of No. 11 Group. Odiham then became part of the jet age and it was home to many jet fighter squadrons during the 1950s; Vampires, Meteors, Hunters and Javelins being amongst the resident squadrons. In

1959 it was decided to close Odiham as a fighter station and the airfield was placed on care and maintenance before the airfield was transferred back to Transport Command in 1960.

Odiham then became home to helicopters, initially Sycamores and Whirlwinds, and then the Wessex and Belvedere before the arrival of the Puma in the early 1970s and ultimately the Chinook ten years later. The airfield can be found to the east of Junction 5 of the M3 by taking the A287 towards Farnham and at the village of Warnborough follow the signs to RAF Odiham to the right. Needless to say, being an active RAF station, prior permission is required if you ever intend to visit.

Squadron	Dates at Odiham	Aircraft type
2 Squadron	10 Aug 43–22 Jan 44	Mustang I
168 Squadron	17 Mar–20 Sep 43	Mustang I
170 Squadron	26 Jun–20 Sep 43	Mustang I
268 Squadron	31 May–15 Sep 43	Mustang I
4 Squadron	7 Aug–15 Sep 43	Mustang I
	6 Oct–15 Nov 43	Mustang I
181 Squadron	31 Dec 43–13 Jan 44	Typhoon I
247 Squadron	31 Dec 43–13 Jan 44	Typhoon I
400 Squadron RCAF	18 Feb–1 Jul 44	Spitfire XI/ Mosquito XVI
414 Squadron RCAF	19–28 Feb 44	Mustang I
184 Squadron	6–11 Mar 44	Typhoon I
	3–23 Apr 44	Typhoon I
168 Squadron	31 Mar–29 Jun 44	Mustang I
414 Squadron RCAF	1 Apr–15 Aug 44	Mustang I
430 Squadron RCAF	1 Apr–29 Jun 44	Mustang I
2 Squadron	27 Jun–30 Jul 44	Mustang II
4 Squadron	27 Jun–16 Aug 44	Spitfire XI
268 Squadron	27 Jun–10 Aug 44	Mustang I
96 Squadron	24 Sep–12 Dec 44	Mosquito XIII
604 Squadron	4–31 Dec 44	Mosquito XIII
264 Squadron	21 Dec 44–8 Jan 45	Mosquito XIII

Thruxton

Located 5 miles to the west of Andover in Hampshire, and right on the county border with Wiltshire, is the former wartime airfield of Thruxton. It is probably now more famous as a racing circuit but Thruxton was once home to tactical reconnaissance Mustangs of the newly formed 2nd TAF.

Thruxton was another site acquired by the Air Ministry during 1940 when the need for airfields in the south of England increased and land was purchased from the Thruxton Manor Estate. The airfield opened during the summer of 1941 and was taken over by Army Co-Operation Command as a satellite for Andover. It initially had three concrete runways, although these were soon relayed with tarmac, which were optimally placed at 60-degree angles to each other. The main runway was over 1,500 yards long and aligned east-west and the two secondary runways were aligned south-east to north-west (1,200 yards) and aligned almost north-south (1,000 yards). The airfield would eventually have nearly thirty hardstandings and six double-aircraft pans enclosed by a standard perimeter track.

The ground support site, where the station headquarters and other key station personnel were located, as well as other facilities such as the various mess facilities, motor transport facilities, briefing huts and supply buildings, as well as a

During late 1943 Mustangs of the newly formed 2nd TAF flew from Thruxton in the tactical reconnaissance role in preparation for the forthcoming Allied invasion of Europe.

The former wartime airfield of Thruxton is dominated today by the motor racing circuit where you can buy a session around the track in high-performance cars.

hospital and a chapel, were all mainly Nissen huts of various sizes, which were all connected by a network of support roads and paths. The technical site consisted of a T-2 hangar and nine Blister hangars, as well as numerous maintenance buildings. An ammunition dump was located on the south-east side of the airfield and outside of the perimeter track, and various domestic sites were constructed and dispersed a short distance away from the airfield, which provided accommodation for Thruxton's personnel.

The first aircraft to use Thruxton were Lysanders, which moved in soon after the airfield opened, after which the airfield was mainly used by Whitleys involved in paratroop exercises and operations, and briefly by Mustangs. Then, in August 1942, Thruxton became home to Bostons and Blenheims, which were engaged in smoke-laying operations to support the seaborne assault on Dieppe, and during early 1943 the Whitleys became increasingly involved in the towing of Horsa gliders.

Following the formation of the 2nd TAF, Mustangs of No. 123 Airfield, part of the newly formed No. 84 Group of the 2nd TAF, moved to Thruxton in October 1942. The three squadrons consisted of Nos 168, 170 and 268 Squadrons, although No. 168 Squadron was soon replaced by No. 63 Squadron, which moved south from Turnhouse the following month. While operating from Thruxton the Mustangs flew tactical reconnaissance sorties

The air traffic control tower is immediately visible as you enter the Thruxton complex.

over northern France in preparation for the forthcoming Allied invasion of Europe but they did not stay long and soon moved to Sawbridgeworth on 12 November. The airfield was then used again to train glider pilots.

From February 1944 Thruxton was home to the Americans of the USAAF and P-47 Thunderbolts flew fighter-bomber missions from the airfield during the build-up to D-Day and during its immediate aftermath. The Thunderbolts moved out soon after D-Day and they were replaced by Avro Ansons, which were used to ferry casualties back from the Normandy beachhead. Once the ferrying of casualties back from northern France was complete, the Ansons were then used for communications purposes. After the airborne assault on north-west Europe was complete, Thruxton then became a storage site for Horsa gliders but at the end of the war these were gradually broken up and the airfield was no longer required by the Air Ministry. After the war the airfield was used for light aircraft flying and gliding, leased by the Wiltshire School of Flying, and during the late 1950s and early 1960s the site was developed as a motor racing and motor bike circuit, complete with viewing stands.

Thruxton is still used as an airfield today and has been operated by Western Air (Thruxton) Limited for the past forty years. Now known as Thruxton Airport there are facilities for hiring aircraft and helicopters as well as learning to fly both types; there are also a number of private aircraft that use the airfield. There is one hardened runway about 800 yards long and a grass runway of similar length. The racing circuit makes use of the old perimeter track around the outside of the site. The south-west end of the former secondary runway, which ran almost north-south, is now used for aircraft parking with other airport facilities also built on the former runway; the northern end of the runway still exists but is mainly used for aircraft parking. Part of the original east-west runway still exists as the main runway and the grass runway was built parallel to the other secondary runway that ran from the south-east to the north-west.

The airfield and racing circuit can be found by following the A303 from Andover towards the south-west and the site is just to the north of the main road and to the west of the village of Thruxton. The best thing is to follow the road signs to the racing circuit from the A303 because of the dual carriageway and do not follow the signs to the village. It is a site worth visiting as there are still some reminders of the former wartime airfield as well as it being a place of interest for the motor racing enthusiast where you can buy a session around the track in high performance cars on a licensed racing circuit.

Some of the former wartime buildings at Thruxton have survived, including a number of Nissen huts and a T2 hangar, and these can be seen by visiting the small industrial estate on the edge of the airfield.

As you arrive at the airfield and racing circuit, you are coming into the western end of the site. A right hand turn at the main entrance takes you down towards the complex. You will soon see a tunnel going underneath the race track into the circuit and to the paddock car park. Before going through the tunnel, stop for a moment to look at the air traffic control tower on your right. Although the tower is not accessible to the public, unless you have made a previous appointment, you can still get a good view across the airfield and racing circuit. If you can get up the tower then even better and, as you would expect, you get a commanding view from there across the whole airfield.

Having then passed through the tunnel you can also get an excellent view of the hardened runway. Many former wartime buildings remain on the site, most notably on the southern part of the airfield, which is now a small industrial estate. If you have permission you can access the area by returning back through the tunnel and away from the complex. Turn left at the T-junction and having then passed a small hangar on your left take the next track to the left. Follow this track for several hundred yards, past a quarried area on your left, and then follow the track round to the left until you arrive at the site of the buildings. Many of these buildings are still in use and so permission to observe them should be attained. Also, please drive carefully to the site and park accordingly before observing the T2 hangar and Nissen huts that still remain.

Squadron	Dates at Thruxton	Aircraft type
168 Squadron	15 Oct–12 Nov 43	Mustang I
170 Squadron	16 Oct–12 Nov 43	Mustang I
268 Squadron	15 Oct–7 Nov 43	Mustang I
63 Squadron	8–12 Nov 43	Mustang I

CHAPTER FIVE

Airfields of the South-West

The south-west of England is one of the most popular parts of Britain; it is certainly a most wonderful place to visit for a variety of reasons, whether it is for its beautiful coastline, its challenging waves or its peaceful atmosphere out of the tourist season. But the area is not always best known for its aviation, although the south-west has been home to many airfields over the years; about 100 in all. The region does have airports that have been developed in recent years from former military establishments, such as Newquay Airport in Cornwall, which has been developed on the site of RAF St Mawgan, once a Coastal Command airfield and home to the Nimrod anti-submarine aircraft.

In terms of determining the boundary of what is considered to be the south-west, those airfields to the west of the Hampshire county border have been included in this chapter. The most eastern of the airfields, Hurn in Dorset, now more familiar to holiday makers and tourists as Bournemouth Airport, needs little or no introduction. With some 200 combat aircraft located at the airfield during June 1944, including two wings of Typhoon fighter-bombers, it was one of the busiest 2nd TAF airfields during D-Day. However, due to their location, far from the invasion beaches, the other two airfields, Zeals and Perranporth, although used by the 2nd TAF during 1943–44, were less busy and are likely to be less familiar names to all but the local villagers or the more knowledgeable RAF historians.

The first, Zeals, is in Wiltshire. As one of Britain's oldest counties, Wiltshire has enjoyed a long association with military aviation since 1912 when the War Office first expressed an interest in the use of aeroplanes for military purposes. Larkhill was first used for a military trial and then two years later, in 1914, the newly formed Royal Flying Corps established its two major airfields at Netheravon and Upavon. A number of military airfields then followed but after the First World War most were closed down. The inter-war years saw new private airfields appear before there was a revival of military aviation in Wiltshire during the 1930s and by the outbreak of the Second World War there were several military airfields in use, although their location in the south-west of England meant that the main airfields at Larkhill, Netheravon and Upavon, were too far away from the operational front line and so they were generally used as training and support establishments. New airfields were then developed to provide support for the Army and they became the centre for airborne forces' parachute and glider training but Zeals was found suitable for operational units and so was used by RAF fighters.

The other airfield covered in this chapter, and the most south-western of all the airfields covered in this series, is Perranporth, which lies on the north Cornwall coast to the south-west of Newquay. Cornwall's natural assets tend to link the county's history with the sea and fishing and its naturally rich minerals such as tin, silver, lead and copper. Indeed, many mining shafts are still visible in the local area today. Perranporth is probably better known more recently for its long sandy beaches, and the airfields of Cornwall are historically better known for operating aircraft of Coastal Command rather than operating fighters; for example, the airfields of St Mawgan, St Eval and Portreath – all located in the surrounding area – were all main bases for Coastal Command during the Battle of the Atlantic. Yet, Perranporth provides us with a good example of one of many fighter airfields built during the Second World War in outlying parts of Britain.

These three airfields – Hurn, Zeals and Perranporth – are the only airfields that were used by 2nd TAF units during the period 1943–44 and, therefore, covered in this chapter. Not included are the airfields or landing grounds that were used extensively by the United States Ninth Air Force, such as Bisterne near Ringwood in Dorset.

Hurn

Located about 4 miles to the north-east of Bournemouth, just to the west of the A338 that runs southwards from Ringwood, is Bournemouth Airport. The site has now been developed beyond all recognition to what it was like in June 1944 and few of the 2nd TAF's airfields were busier than Hurn when two Typhoon wings, each of three squadrons, and two squadrons of Mosquitos made a total of more than 200 combat aircraft operating from the airfield during the D-Day operations.

Soon after the start of the Second World War the area had been identified as suitable to develop a satellite airfield for Ibsley. Work began during 1940 and Hurn opened in July 1941. The airfield consisted of three hardened runways; the main runway, which ran from east–west was some 2,000 yards in length, with a second runway running north–south of 1,600 yards and the third runway of 1,100 yards running from the south-east to the north-west. Hardstandings were constructed off the perimeter track in a loop connecting the runways. Eventually the technical site would consist of four main T-2 hangars, three Belman hangars and ten Blister hangars, and there was an ammunition dump on the northern side of the airfield outside of the perimeter track. The main administrative site was situated in the north-west part of the airfield and buildings were mainly Nissen huts of various sizes, and a number of domestic sites were constructed near the airfield to accommodate the station personnel, which at its height during the war was some 2,500 people.

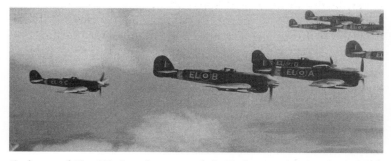

Typhoons of No. 181 Squadron, one of six Typhoon units that formed Nos 124 and 143 Wings at Hurn during the period of the D-Day operations and making Hurn one of the busiest of all the 2nd TAF's airfields in June 1944.

Initially the airfield was not used to any great extent but during 1942 it was developed for the Army Air Corps. Then in March 1944 Hurn was transferred to No. 11 Group. The first fighter-bomber wing to move to Hurn was No. 143 (RCAF) Airfield, consisting of three Canadian Typhoon squadrons, which moved south from Ayr in Scotland during mid-March. Nos 438, 439 and 440 Squadrons RCAF had originally been numbered Nos 118, 123 and 111 Squadrons RCAF respectively. The squadrons' personnel had crossed the Atlantic from their former bases in Canada just a matter of weeks earlier and all three squadrons had initially been equipped with Hurricane IVs but were now taking delivery of the Typhoon fighter-bomber.

Commanding No. 143 Airfield was the Canadian Wing Commander Frank Hillock with the Typhoons led by the Canadian Wing Commander Flying, Wing Commander Bob Davidson, a veteran of the Greece, Western Desert and Far East campaigns. The wing commenced operations from Hurn on 20 March and, apart from a two-week period in early April, when the wing detached to Funtington to carry out dive-bombing training, the wing continued with fighter-bomber sweeps across the Channel during which the Typhoons carried out attacks on enemy communications targets, coastal radar sites, V-1 flying bomb sites and other key installations in northern France. By now the Canadians had been joined by the Typhoons of No. 124 Airfield – Nos 181, 182 and 247 Squadrons – which had moved to Hurn from Merston on 1 April and led by Wing Commander B G Carroll with the Norwegian Wing Commander Erik Haabjörn as Wing Commander Flying.

It would be these two Typhoon wings that would operate from Hurn during the build-up to the Allied invasion of Europe, with No. 124 Airfield concentrating more on rocket attacks against enemy troop positions and camps, as well as other key targets, in preparation for its army support role during the invasion, while the bomb-carrying Typhoons of No. 143 Airfield were then given a secondary role of smoke-laying, using smoke canisters under each wing, and during April and May the pilots carried out a number of exercises with the Army, although the wing never carried out this role operationally.

Hurn suffered a loss on 8 May when Bob Davidson had to force-land his Typhoon near Béthune. Davidson had been leading No. 438 Squadron during a dive-bombing raid against railway marshalling yards when his engine had cut out. Having force-landed, Davidson evaded capture and was taken in by the local French Resistance and many weeks later he was able to return to Allied hands. Davidson was replaced as wing leader by Wing Commander Mike Judd, a former graduate of Oxford University and an experienced fighter pilot having flown Kittyhawks in North Africa as the commanding officer of No. 250 Squadron, for which he was awarded the DFC after his third kill of the campaign. Now back in the UK, he would command the Typhoons of No. 141 Wing throughout the period of the D-Day operations and subsequently during the Allied advance deeper into Europe.

On 9 May, Erik Haabjörn took more than twenty Typhoons to Manston in Kent, and from there in the afternoon led a long-range fighter sweep to the Knocke-Rheims area. Unfortunately for Haabjörn, his Typhoon suffered an engine failure soon after take-off and he spent the next hour or so in the Channel while the rest of his formation proceeded to the target; Haabjörn would require rescuing again just a matter of days later when he was hit by flak while operating in the Dieppe area and had to make a second forced landing into the sea. Another Hurn pilot to be rescued from the sea was Squadron Leader Jimmy Keep, the officer commanding No. 181 Squadron, who ditched his Typhoon near Cherbourg during the late afternoon of 23 May. Keep was rescued but his injuries meant that he was taken off operations and he was replaced as the squadron commander by one of the flight commanders serving with No. 182 Squadron, 'Kit' North-Lewis, who was immediately promoted and posted across the airfield to his new squadron.

Also based at Hurn during this period were the night-fighter Mosquitos of Nos 125 and 604 Squadrons, part of No. 85 Group, which meant that more than 200 combat aircraft were now operating from the airfield, making Hurn one of the busiest airfields in southern England. In addition to their main role as night-fighters, which saw some success while operating from Hurn, the squadrons took part in various operations supporting the build-up to D-Day such as carrying out decoy operations by dropping 'Window' across the Channel.

For the D-Day operations the Mosquitos were airborne during the night of 5/6 June to provide night-fighter cover for the Allied forces. Then, during the early morning of D-Day, the Typhoons of the Canadian No. 143 Wing were amongst the first Allied aircraft to carry out attacks against enemy defensive positions as the first landing craft went ashore at 7.30 a.m. Their targets were pre-planned and included the key defensive positions opposing the landings at Gold beach, at Le Hamel and La Rivière, on Juno at Courseulles and at Hermanville opposing the landings at Sword beach. During the late afternoon a Typhoon of No. 181 Squadron, flown by twenty-two years old Australian Flight Sergeant George Howard was shot down near Caen and Hurn suffered a further loss during the evening when a Typhoon of No. 440 Squadron was shot down by flak while carrying out a sortie near the Falaise-Conde road and crashed near Mauvieu; the pilot, twenty-four-year-old Canadian Flying Officer Leonard Allman, was killed.

The day after D-Day proved to be a mixed day for the Hurn squadrons. For some it was a quieter day as the weather started to deteriorate, although the full impact of the deterioration did not hit the Normandy area for another two days. After the intense activity of the day before, some squadron pilots found themselves sitting around and waiting, albeit at a high state of readiness either at cockpit ready or in dispersal. No. 438 Squadron, for example, maintained four aircraft at runway readiness and a further six aircraft on three-minute readiness in the dispersal for most of the day. Other Hurn squadrons, however, were busy and during the morning there were further losses for No. 440 Squadron when three Typhoons were shot down by flak to the south of Caen; twenty-four-year-old Flying Officer Stanley Garside from Edmonton in Alberta and Flying Officer Wilfred Mahagan from Ontario were both killed. The third pilot shot down, Flying Officer Ronald Doidge, had a lucky escape having baled out and survived. He evaded capture and later returned to the squadron but sadly Ronald Doidge would later be killed during October while serving with the squadron over Holland. Then during the evening of 8 June the Typhoons were again operating over the invasion area, this time attacking enemy armoured vehicles around Caen, when two of the Typhoons were hit by flak, although both pilots were able to make emergency landings in territory occupied by the Allies. It was a hazardous time for the Typhoon squadrons.

The weather then deteriorated on 9 June, which resulted in a significant reduction in Allied sorties flown and at times brought air operations to a halt. Better weather saw operations resume and the following day thirty Typhoons of No. 124 Wing joined forces with ten Typhoons of No. 245 Squadron from Holmsley South, and more than seventy Mitchells of No. 2 Group, to carry out a most successful attack against the headquarters of the commander of Panzergruppe West, General Geyr von Schweppenburg, located in the Chateau de la Caine to the south-west of Caen. Poor weather had meant that the raid had been delayed from the morning until the early evening but the Typhoons, each armed with eight 60lb rockets, carried out a devastating attack from 2,000 feet, which resulted in the destruction of the headquarters, including vital communications and signals equipment, as well as the destruction of a number of vehicles located in the grounds of the chateau. So successful was the raid that it would be more than two weeks before the headquarters would be fully functional again.

In the late morning of 13 June the Typhoons of No. 124 Wing flew across the Channel to the newly prepared landing strip at Banville (B.2); the idea was for the Typhoons to then conduct operations from across the Channel during the rest of the day before returning to Hurn at dusk. During the following nights both Hurn Mosquito squadrons enjoyed some success by shooting down a number of enemy aircraft. By mid-June the need for night support had decreased and No. 604 squadron left Hurn for Colerne. No. 125 Squadron remained at Hurn but was now increasingly taking part in anti-Diver patrols over southern England to counter the increasing V-1 flying bomb threat.

The Hurn Typhoon wings of No. 83 Group had flown relentlessly during the final weeks before D-Day and the period immediately after. Amongst their great successes there had also been losses, particularly when attacking well defended German armoured units that were moving up to the battle area as reinforcements. No. 124 Wing was then amongst the first Allied combat aircraft to cross the Channel to operate in northern France, leaving Hurn for Coulombs (B.6) on 20 June. The wing was replaced at Hurn by another Typhoon wing, No. 136 Wing, consisting of another three squadrons; two of the squadrons – Nos 164 and 198 Squadrons – arrived from Funtington and the third, No. 609 Squadron, returned back from across the Channel where it had briefly operated from Bazenville (B.2), although a week later the squadron would leave Hurn and cross the Channel once more; this time to operate from Plumetot (B.10).

On the day No. 198 Squadron arrived at Hurn, 22 June, the squadron suffered the loss of its new commanding officer, Squadron Leader I J Davies, who had only taken over command of the squadron two weeks earlier. Davies was shot down during the early afternoon while providing air support for American forces on the ground near Cherbourg. Although he was seen to have baled out of his aircraft, Davies was clearly too low and his parachute had failed to deploy completely.

By the end of June the Canadian wing had also crossed the Channel to provide air support for the advancing Allied ground forces from their new home at Lantheuil (B.9). More Typhoons arrived at Hurn and the airfield was soon home to a number of Typhoons from all three Typhoon wings of No. 84 Group – Nos 123, 136 and 146 Wings – with all four squadrons of No. 146 Wing – Nos 193, 197, 257 and 266 Squadrons –arriving at Hurn during the first week of July. Hurn was an extremely busy airfield and there were periods when up to ten squadrons were operating from the airfield, as well as two Mosquito squadrons, at any one time. Gradually, however, the squadrons crossed the

The former wartime airfield of Hurn is now Bournemouth Airport.

Channel to operate from landing strips in northern France and by the end of July all the Typhoon squadrons had gone.

Hurn was then used briefly by the USAAF, after which the airfield was transferred to the Ministry of Civil Aviation. Before long, airlines such as BOAC, Pan Am, KLM and Sabena were all operating regular commercial routes from the airport to destinations across the world. The opening of London Airport soon after the end of the war saw a reduction in commercial operators during the next ten years and although there were many times when the airfield came close to closure it carried on during the following decades. In 1969 the airport was purchased by Dorset County Council and the Bournemouth Corporation and renamed as Bournemouth Airport, which later became

Squadron	Dates at Hurn	Aircraft type
438 Squadron RCAF	18 Mar – 3 Apr 44	Typhoon I
439 Squadron RCAF	18 Mar – 2 Apr 44	Typhoon I
440 Squadron RCAF	14 Mar – 2 Apr 44	Typhoon I
125 Squadron	25 Mar – 30 Jul 44	Mosquito XVII
181 Squadron	1 Apr – 20 Jun 44	Typhoon I
182 Squadron	1 Apr – 20 Jun 44	Typhoon I
247 Squadron	24 Apr – 20 Jun 44	Typhoon I
438 Squadron RCAF	20 Apr – 27 Jun 44	Typhoon I
439 Squadron RCAF	19 Apr – 27 Jun 44	Typhoon I
440 Squadron RCAF	19 Apr – 27 Jun 44	Typhoon I
604 Squadron	2 May – 13 Jun 44	Mosquito XII / XIII
164 Squadron	21 Jun – 17 Jul 44	Typhoon I
198 Squadron	22 Jun – 1 Jul 44	Typhoon I
609 Squadron	22 Jun – 1 Jul 44	Typhoon I
183 Squadron	22 Jun – 14 Jul 44	Typhoon I
193 Squadron	3 – 11 Jul 44	Typhoon I
197 Squadron	3 – 17 Jul 44	Typhoon I
257 Squadron	2 – 15 Jul 44	Typhoon I
266 Squadron	13 – 17 Jul 44	Typhoon I

Bournemouth International Airport. The runway was extended during the mid-1990s and in 2001 the airport was acquired by the Manchester Airports Group, the largest UK-owned airport group. In 2007 the owners announced a large investment in the redevelopment of the airport and major work began the following year and continues to the present day.

The airport is easy to find and is situated on the north-western edge of Hurn village, which is about 4 miles to the north-east of Bournemouth. It can be found from the A338 in either direction. Take the B3073 through the village of Hurn and then continue left, remaining on the B3073 Parley Lane, until you come to a set of traffic lights; the entrance to the airport is on the right. If you continue along the B3073 the road takes you along the southern edge of the airport and then continues around the western edge.

Perranporth
On the north Cornwall coast, just to the south-west of the village of Perranporth and on top of the cliffs overlooking the sea is the furthest west of all the airfields used by the 2nd TAF during the Second World War. The airfield of Perranporth was developed early in 1941 as a satellite for Portreath when it became apparent that the Second World War would become a war of attrition and it was deemed necessary to protect the vital south-western approaches to Britain. The airfield's facilities were basic as it was only ever intended for use by one squadron at a time. Its three runways were joined by a perimeter track, linking a number of blast pens to allow the dispersal of fighters. The technical buildings included a number of small hangars for maintenance but all domestic accommodation was off site.

The first aircraft to arrive were Spitfires, which provided coastal defensive patrols to cover the vulnerable south-west approaches. Fighter sweeps across the Channel were later introduced and the number of resident squadrons at times peaked at three, which led to the runways being extended and the construction of more buildings. A Polish wing of two Spitfire squadrons – Nos 302 and 317 Squadrons – arrived in June 1943. However, the runways were never long enough to allow fighter-bombers, such as bomb-carrying Typhoons, to operate from the airfield. Typhoons of No. 183 Squadron did arrive at Perranporth in September 1943 to carry out missions across the Channel,

Situated on the north Cornwall coast, on top of the cliffs overlooking the sea, Perranporth was the furthest west of all the 2nd TAF airfields used during the Second World War but has survived to the present day and is now used for light aircraft flying.

specifically in and around the area of the Brest Peninsula, but the restriction of not being able to carry bombs meant that the squadron soon moved out to Predannack.

By the beginning of 1944 there were three French squadrons of Spitfires – Nos 329, 340 and 341 Squadrons – making up No. 145 Wing at Perranporth. The wing provided convoy patrols over the south-western approaches before moving to Merston as No. 145 Airfield in April, where the squadrons would be closer to the planned invasion area and from where they would operate during the D-Day period.

Perranporth was then transferred to Coastal Command and the airfield used by Fleet Air Arm squadrons for operations against the German E-boats operating in the area, which continued until July after which the squadrons left Perranporth and the airfield was placed on care and maintenance. The airfield was briefly used during the latter months of 1944 and early months of 1945 before it was once again placed on care and maintenance at the end of the war. In 1946 the airfield was closed by the Air Ministry and the site was later returned to agriculture but its location on top of the cliffs and the prevailing westerly winds made Perranporth ideal for gliding. By the end of the 1950s, Perranporth was one of the busiest gliding sites in the country.

Next to the air traffic control tower is a memorial to all those who flew from Perranporth during the war.

Since then there have been plans to expand the use of the airfield but opposition has prevented any further development.

Perranporth has survived until the present day and is currently an active airfield used for light aircraft flying. Some of the airfield's permanent facilities have survived despite the fact that the site was required for agriculture during the post-war period and there appears to have been little, if any, post-war building construction. The airfield lies to the south of Perranporth on the B3285 towards St Agnes. When approaching from either Perranporth or St Agnes, you will need to drive to the village of Trevellas and then follow the signpost to the aerodrome, which is about half a mile to the west of the village, towards the coast. If approaching Trevellas from the A30, it is not so easy to find and some of the roads are extremely narrow with few passing places. When at the site take care due to the close proximity of the aircraft. The fact that it is an active airfield will prevent you from walking over the site unless you have prior permission. You can, however, view the original air traffic control tower and the memorial to those who flew from the airfield during the Second World War. You will also get a good view across the airfield and watch any local flying that is taking place.

Squadron	Dates at Perranporth	Aircraft type
302 'Poznanski' Squadron	20 Jun–19 Aug 43	Spitfire V
317 'Wilenski' Squadron	21 Jun–21 Aug 43	Spitfire V
183 Squadron	18 Sep–13 Oct 43	Typhoon I
453 Squadron RAAF	21 Aug–18 Oct 43	Spitfire V
340 (Free French) Squadron	9 Nov 43–17 Apr 44	Spitfire V
341 (Free French) Squadron	15 Oct 43–17 Apr 44	Spitfire V
329 (Free French) Squadron	22 Jan–17 Apr 44	Spitfire V

Zeals

Just to the north of the A303 on the county border of Wiltshire and Somerset, between Amesbury and Wincanton, is the site of the wartime airfield of Zeals, once home to Mosquito night-fighters during 1944. It was the most south-western of more than thirty Wiltshire military airfields used during the Second World War and was opened in May 1942 as a forward operating airfield of No. 10 Group, Fighter Command.

After the Second World War the airfield of Zeals was transferred to the Admiralty as HMS Humming Bird, *a Fleet Air Arm training station, and was used by a number of FAA units with the role of providing target aircraft, such as Fireflies, for the training of fighter controllers. (Yvonne Durell)*

181

The airfield was developed on 500 acres of grassland adjacent to Zeals Knoll on the western edge of Salisbury Plain and just a mile to the north of Zeals village. The natural features of the local area included a steep-sided valley to the west of the site and sloping land towards the south-east. Although the airfield was grass, a fair amount of construction work was completed during the following year, including a tarmac perimeter track, nine hangars and domestic accommodation. There were three runways at 60-degree angles to each other. One essentially ran from east to west, one from the south-east to the north-west and a third ran from the south-west to the north-east, with a tarmac perimeter track connecting them all from which were constructed thirty aircraft dispersals and eight Blister hangars. In the south-east part of the airfield was the technical site with a T-1 hangar. The administrative site and domestic sites were all located in the local area near the village of Zeals, although it was some time before the airfield facilities were complete and initially, for the first year at least, the facilities at the airfield were quite basic with many of the station personnel living in tents.

The minor road connecting the village of Zeals with the nearby village of Stourton had to be closed for the development of the airfield. The first aircraft to make use of Zeals were Hurricanes and Defiants of No. 286 Squadron, which were used for target-towing and gun-laying training for the anti-aircraft defences in the south-west of England. During the following months the airfield was home to two squadrons of Spitfire Vs of the Ibsley Wing, which carried out bomber escort duties, often for Bostons of No. 2 Group, and they also took part in fighter sweeps across the Channel. However, poor drainage of the grass airfield following periods of heavy rain meant that operations from Zeals were not possible during the winter months and the Spitfires moved out in December.

Flying resumed in March 1943 when two squadrons of Hurricane IIs and one squadron of Spitfire Vs of No. 122 Airfield spent two weeks at Zeals working closely with the Army as part of Exercise *Spartan*, an early attempt to co-ordinate land and air assets as part of joint operations. Once the exercise had finished the squadrons moved out and attempts were then made to improve the drainage before the airfield was made available to elements of the USAAF, initially with the intent of using

The former air traffic control tower at Zeals remained in a derelict state long after the end of the Second World War. It is pictured here in 1964. (Kevin Byrne)

the airfield for American transport aircraft. However, the poor drainage now meant that the airfield was not suitable for use by transport aircraft and so American P-47 Thunderbolts moved in but further problems with drainage then meant that operations from Zeals were not possible.

The airfield constructors moved in once more to build aircraft hardstandings and to lay Sommerfeld tracking for runways but a particularly wet winter meant there was little air activity until Zeals resumed flying operations in April 1944 under the control of No. 10 Group. The following month Mosquito night-fighters of No. 488 Squadron, a unit allocated to the 2nd TAF, moved into Zeals from Bradwell Bay to counter the nuisance bombing raids carried out by the Luftwaffe over the south-west of England.

Facilities at Zeals were then improved to allow night-fighter operations and the Mosquitos were soon in action. One pilot to enjoy early success from Zeals was twenty-two-year-old Flight Lieutenant John Hall. Born in Oxford, Hall had joined No. 488 Squadron in November 1943. Flying with his radar operator, Flying Officer 'Jock' Cairns, on the night of 14/15 May Hall shot

The air traffic control tower today having been converted into a private residence called Tower House.

down a Junkers Ju188 to the north-east of Exeter. This was the crew's fifth success together on the squadron for which they were both awarded the DFC the following month. By the end of the war both John Hall and 'Jock' Cairns would receive a bar to their DFCs for eight confirmed kills.

No. 488 Squadron remained at Zeals during the build-up to D-Day, and on D-Day itself when the squadron provided night cover over the Normandy beachhead. The squadron was then paired up with a second Mosquito night-fighter squadron, No. 604 Squadron, based at Colerne and led by the night-fighter ace, Wing Commander Michael Constable-Maxwell, and the two squadrons operated together as No. 147 Wing.

The night-fighter Mosquitos of No. 85 Group, including three crews of No. 147 Wing, enjoyed considerable success on the night of 12/13 June when nine Luftwaffe bombers were shot down. Two aircraft were shot down by No. 604 Squadron – a Heinkel He177 and a Junkers Ju88 – and one by No. 488 Squadron, another Junkers Ju88 shot down by the night-fighter ace Squadron Leader Nigel Bunting, one of the squadron's flight commanders who had already been credited with seven kills and had been awarded the DFC. Four nights later there was a further success for No. 488 Squadron when Bunting and his radar operator, Flight Lieutenant Reed, shot down a Focke-Wulf FW190 to the south of St Lô; it was Bunting's ninth success of the war and it brought him and his radar operator a bar to their DFCs. Sadly, however, the crew would not survive the war as they were shot down over Normandy on the night of 30/31 July 1944; and both men were killed.

No. 488 Squadron was then joined at Zeals by a second night-fighter unit, No. 410 Squadron, which arrived from Hunsdon on 18 June, and these two squadrons now operated as No. 149 Wing. One of the most successful night-fighter pilots to have flown from Zeals during the D-Day period was twenty-two-year-old Flight Lieutenant 'Jamie' Jameson, the top-scoring New Zealand night-fighter ace of the war. Jameson had joined the RNZAF in February 1941 and following his pilot training was posted to the UK. He had claimed three victories by early 1943 with No. 125 Squadron, for which he was awarded the DFC, and was then posted to No. 488 Squadron in January 1944. He went on to achieve considerable success with his radar operator, Flying Officer Norman Crookes. While at Zeals he added two more to his total; a Messerschmitt Me410 to the south-west of Bayeux on the night of 24/25 June and a Junkers Ju88 to the north-east of Caen four nights later. Jameson would go on to be credited with eleven confirmed kills, including four in one night on 29/30 July, for which he was also awarded the DSO.

Another night of success for the Mosquitos of Zeals was the night of 8/9 July when Squadron Leader March and Flight Lieutenant Eyolfson of No. 410 Squadron shot down a Messerschmitt Me410 twin-engine fighter near Paris. They also reported seeing another Mosquito from the squadron, flown by Flight Lieutenant Stanley Huppert and Flying Officer Christie, shoot down a Junkers Ju88 before the Mosquito itself was shot down; sadly, the Canadian Stanley Huppert was killed and he is commemorated on the Runnymede Memorial in Surrey.

At the end of July the Mosquito wing left Zeals for Colerne. During its stay No. 488 Squadron had been particularly successful, accounting for more than forty enemy aircraft since its arrival back in May. On the same day that No. 149 Wing left, No. 286 Squadron returned to Zeals from Colerne. The squadron remained for two months during which it operated a variety of aircraft, such as Hurricanes and Martinets, to support anti-aircraft units across the south-western counties.

After the squadron had moved out, Zeals was then home to a glider training school before the airfield was transferred to

Tower House overlooks the former airfield of Zeals, which reverted to agriculture after the war.

the Admiralty in April 1945 as HMS *Humming Bird*, a Fleet Air Arm training station. The airfield was then used by a number of FAA units with the role of providing target aircraft such as Fireflies and Seafires for the training of fighter control directors. However, all the former problems of drainage remained and by the end of the year all the FAA units had moved out. The airfield was then placed on care and maintenance, after which the land reverted to agriculture. Over the years the perimeter track at the western edge of the former airfield has been used by light aircraft for agricultural crop spraying and some of the domestic buildings on the southern part of the airfield have survived. The former air traffic control tower has since been converted to a private residence known as Tower House.

The site of the former airfield can be found by taking the A303 south-westwards towards Wincanton. Soon after passing the first exit to the village of Mere on the A303, take the B3092 northwards towards the village of Stourton. Just after taking the B3092 take the left turn towards the village of Zeals. After about a mile, and just as you enter the village, take the first narrow lane on the right. This lane, called Bells Lane, heads north towards Stourton and runs parallel to the B3092 that you left earlier. After passing through an area of some residential properties you will see Tower House on your left and you can now get a view northwards across the site of the former airfield, although a line of trees running approximately half way across the former airfield have somewhat changed the sense of size. The east–west runway was just in front of Tower House. If you continue along the lane and pass the trees, you will find some crossroads where a lane running east-west marks the northern part of the former airfield. A memorial stands in Stourton to mark the site where a DC-3 Dakota transport aircraft crashed in 1945 killing more than twenty people.

Squadron	Dates at Zeals	Aircraft type
488 Squadron RNZAF	11 May–28 Jul 44	Mosquito XIII
410 Squadron RCAF	18 Jun–28 Jul 44	Mosquito XIII
286 Squadron	28 Jul–28 Sep 44	Hurricane II, Martinet I

The 2nd TAF Orbat – 30 November 1943

2nd TAF Headquarters

34 Wing	Hartford Bridge	
	No. 16 Sqn	Spitfire XI
	No. 140 Sqn	Spitfire XI

No. 2 Group

Headquarters – Bylaugh Hall, East Dereham

No. 137 Airfield	Hartford Bridge	No. 88 Sqn	Boston III
		No. 107 Sqn	Boston III
		No. 342 Sqn	Boston III
No. 138 Airfield	Lasham	No. 320 Sqn	Mitchell II
		No. 613 Sqn	Mosquito VI
No. 139 Airfield	Dunsfold	No. 98 Sqn	Mitchell II
		No. 180 Sqn	Mitchell II
No. 140 Airfield	Sculthorpe	No. 21 Sqn	Mosquito VI
		No. 464 Sqn	Mosquito VI
		No. 487 Sqn	Mosquito VI
No designated number	Swanton Morley	No. 226 Sqn	Mitchell II

No. 83 Group

Headquarters – Gatton Park, Reigate

No. 15 Wing	No. 122 Airfield	Gravesend	No. 19 Sqn	Spitfire IX
			No. 65 Sqn	Spitfire IX
			No. 122 Sqn	Spitfire IX
	No. 125 Airfield	Detling	No. 132 Sqn	Spitfire IX
			No. 184 Sqn	Hurricane IV
			No. 602 Sqn	Spitfire IX
No. 16 Wing	No. 121 Airfield	Westhampnett	No. 174 Sqn	Typhoon I
			No. 175 Sqn	Typhoon I
			No. 245 Sqn	Typhoon I
	No. 124 Airfield	Merston	No. 181 Sqn	Typhoon I
			No. 182 Sqn	Typhoon I
			No. 247 Sqn	Typhoon I
No. 17 Wing	No. 126 Airfield	Biggin Hill	No. 401 Sqn	Spitfire IX
			No. 411 Sqn	Spitfire V
			No. 412 Sqn	Spitfire IX
	No. 127 Airfield	Kenley	No. 403 Sqn	Spitfire IX
			No. 421 Sqn	Spitfire IX
	No. 128 Airfield	Redhill	No. 231 Sqn	Mustang I
			No. 400 Sqn	Mustang I
	No. 129 Airfield	Gatwick	No. 414 Sqn	Mustang I
			No. 430 Sqn	Mustang I

In addition, there were four Army Observation Post Squadrons allocated to No. 83 Group. These squadrons were equipped with Auster IIIs and were: No. 653 Sqn (Penshurst), No. 658 Sqn (Clifton), No. 659 Sqn (Clifton) and No. 662 Sqn (Old Sarum).

No. 84 Group

Headquarters – Cowley Barracks, Oxford

No. 18 Wing	No. 131 Airfield Northolt	No. 302 Sqn	Spitfire IX
		No. 308 Sqn	Spitfire IX
		No. 317 Sqn	Spitfire IX
	No. 133 Airfield Heston	No. 306 Sqn	Spitfire V
		No. 315 Sqn	Spitfire V
No. 19 Wing	No. 132 Airfield North Weald	No. 331 Sqn	Spitfire IX
		No. 332 Sqn	Spitfire IX
	No. 134 Airfield Ibsley	No. 310 Sqn	Spitfire V
		No. 312 Sqn	Spitfire V
		No. 313 Sqn	Spitfire V

No. 20 Wing	No. 135 Airfield Hornchurch	No. 66 Sqn	Spitfire IX
		No. 129 Sqn	Spitfire IX
		No. 350 Sqn	Spitfire IX
	No. 136 Airfield Fairlop	No. 164 Sqn	Hurricane IV
		No. 195 Sqn	Typhoon I
	No. 123 Airfield Thruxton	No. 63 Sqn	Mustang I
		No. 168 Sqn	Mustang I
		No. 170 Sqn	Mustang I
	No. 130 Airfield Odiham	No. 2 Sqn	Mustang I
		No. 4 Sqn	Mustang I

In addition, there were three Army Observation Post Squadrons allocated to No. 84 Group. These squadrons were equipped with Auster IIIs and were: No. 652 Sqn (Ipswich), No. 660 Sqn (Hammerwood House) and No. 661 Sqn (Andover).

The 2nd TAF Orbat –
6 June 1944

2nd TAF Headquarters
34 (PR) Wing Northolt

No. 16 Sqn	Spitfire XI
No. 69 Sqn	Wellington XIII
No. 140 Sqn	Mosquito XVI

In addition, No. 1401 (Met) Flight based at Manston

No. 2 Group

No. 137 Wing	Hartford Bridge	No. 88 Sqn	Boston III
		No. 226 Sqn	Mitchell II
		No. 342 Sqn	Boston III
No. 138 Wing	Lasham	No. 107 Sqn	Mosquito VI
		No. 305 Sqn	Mosquito VI
		No. 613 Sqn	Mosquito VI
No. 139 Wing	Dunsfold	No. 98 Sqn	Mitchell II
		No. 180 Sqn	Mitchell II
		No. 320 Sqn	Mitchell II
No. 140 Wing	Hunsdon	No. 21 Sqn	Mosquito VI
		No. 464 Sqn	Mosquito VI
		No. 487 Sqn	Mosquito VI

No. 83 Group

No. 121 Wing	Holmsley South	No. 174 Sqn	Typhoon I
		No. 175 Sqn	
		No. 245 Sqn	
No. 122 Wing	Funtington	No. 19 Sqn	Mustang III
		No. 65 Sqn	
		No. 122 Sqn	
No. 124 Wing	Hurn	No. 181 Sqn	Typhoon I
		No. 182 Sqn	
		No. 247 Sqn	
No. 143 Wing		No. 438 Sqn	
		No. 439 Sqn	
		No. 440 Sqn	
No. 125 Wing	Ford	No. 132 Sqn	Spitfire IX
		No. 453 Sqn	
		No. 602 Sqn	
No. 144 Wing		No. 441 Sqn	
		No. 442 Sqn	
		No. 443 Sqn	
No. 126 Wing	Tangmere	No. 401 Sqn	Spitfire IX
		No. 411 Sqn	
		No. 412 Sqn	
No. 127 Wing		No. 403 Sqn	
		No. 416 Sqn	
		No. 421 Sqn	
No. 129 Wing	Westhampnett	No. 184 Sqn	Typhoon I
No. 39 (PR) Wing	Odiham	No. 168 Sqn	Mustang I
		No. 414 Sqn	
		No. 430 Sqn	
		No. 400 Sqn	Spitfire XI

In addition, there were four Army Observation Post squadrons allocated to No. 83 Group. These squadrons were equipped with Auster IVs and were: No. 653 Sqn (Penshurst), No. 658 Sqn (Old Sarum), No. 659 Sqn (East Grinstead) and No. 662 Sqn (Old Sarum).

No. 84 Group

No. 123 Wing	Thorney Island	No. 198 Sqn	Typhoon I
		No. 609 Sqn	
No. 136 Wing		No. 164 Sqn	
		No. 184 Sqn	
No. 131 Wing	Chailey	No. 302 Sqn	Spitfire IX
		No. 308 Sqn	
		No. 317 Sqn	
No. 132 Wing	Bognor Regis	No. 66 Sqn	Spitfire IX
		No. 331 Sqn	
		No. 332 Sqn	
No. 133 Wing	Coolham	No. 129 Sqn	Mustang III
		No. 306 Sqn	
		No. 315 Sqn	
No. 134 Wing	Appledram	No. 310 Sqn	Spitfire IX
		No. 312 Sqn	
		No. 313 Sqn	
No. 135 Wing	Selsey	No. 222 Sqn	Spitfire IX
		No. 349 Sqn	
		No. 485 Sqn	
No. 145 Wing	Merston	No. 329 Sqn	Spitfire IX
		No. 340 Sqn	
		No. 341 Sqn	
No. 146 Wing	Needs Oar Point	No. 193 Sqn	Typhoon I
		No. 197 Sqn	
		No. 257 Sqn	
		No. 266 Sqn	
No. 35 (Recce) Wing	Gatwick	No. 2 Sqn	Mustang I
		No. 268 Sqn	
		No. 4 Sqn	Spitfire XI

In addition, there were three Army Observation Post squadrons allocated to No. 84 Group. These squadrons were equipped with Auster IVs and were: No. 652 Sqn (Cobham), No. 660 Sqn (Westenhanger) and No. 661 Sqn (Biggin Hill and Fairchildes).

No. 85 Group

No. 141 Wing	Hartford Bridge	No. 264 Sqn	Mosquito XIII
		No. 410 Sqn	
		No. 322 Sqn	Spitfire XIV
No. 142 Wing	Horne	No. 124 Sqn	Spitfire IX
No. 147 Wing	Zeals	No. 488 Sqn	Mosquito XIII
		No. 604 Sqn	
No. 148 Wing	West Malling	No. 29 Sqn	Mosquito XIII
		No. 409 Sqn	
		No. 91 Sqn	Spitfire XIV
No. 150 Wing	Newchurch	No. 3 Sqn	Tempest V
		No. 486 Sqn	
		No. 56 Sqn	Spitfire IX

In addition, there were two RAF Air Spotting Pool squadrons allocated to No. 85 Group. The two RAF squadrons were No. 26 Sqn and No. 63 Sqn, equipped with Spitfire Vs and based at Lee-on-Solent. Also based at Lee-on-Solent for this task were various Fleet Air Arm squadrons.